Palm Beach

COUNTY

In a Class by Itself

Copperfield Publications, Inc.

Published by COPPERFIELD PUBLICATIONS, INC.
2601 East Oakland Park Boulevard, Suite 401
Fort Lauderdale, Florida 33306

Art direction, design and production by Christine Spencer-Bates
Assistant Editor Cheryl Badeaux

Produced in cooperation with the
Judge Knott Center for Historic Preservation

First edition

Library of Congress Catalog Number: 97-69555

ISBN: 0-9647106-2-5
Printed in Korea
Photo this page C. J. Walker

Front cover photo courtesy of:
Henry Morrison Flagler Museum
Photographer: Lucien Capehart

Front cover design by Pearl & Associates

Photo: The Palm Beach Post/Bob Shanley

Table of Contents

ACKNOWLEDGMENTS   7

INTRODUCTION   9

CHAPTER 1   12
The Early Days

CHAPTER 2   42
The Riches of the Land

CHAPTER 3   60
Business Finance & Trade

CHAPTER 4   70
Health Care in Palm Beach County

CHAPTER 5   82
The Power of Education

CHAPTER 6   96
Breaking the News

CHAPTER 7   106
The Finer Things of Life

CHAPTER 8   124
The Good Life

CHAPTER 9   148
From Flagler to "The Best of Everything"

CHAPTER 10   168
Palm Beach County's Enterprise

Acknowledgments

The publisher and editor wish to thank the many people who helped with specific questions and general research for this work. We also thank the many people who over the years have shared their knowledge and research with the editor. Among these are Nan Dennison, Maxine Banash, and Susan Duncan, former directors of the Historical Society of Palm Beach County, Clemmer Mayhew, the society's archivist, Judge James R. Knott, its president emeritus, and former presidents Mary C. Linehan and James Ponce. From the Boca Raton Historical Society, Peggy McCall, volunteer archivist, has always been available for questions, to give advice, and to help with research. We also appreciate the aid of Kristen Hamre, the society's director, Katherine Dickenson, its chairman, Eunice Canty, former chairman, and Cynthia Brown, the president. For their kind help we also thank John Blades of the Henry Morrison Flagler Museum and Will Ray and Deborah S. Hurd and Glen Miller of the Palm Beach County Cultural Council, Dale Hopkins and The Breakers, Boca Raton Resort and Club, Four Seasons Resort, Palm Beach County Sports Commission, Columbia JFK Medical Center, Intracoastal Healthcare Systems, Inc., Norton Museum, The Palm Beach Post, The Weitz Company, Inc., Florida Atlantic University, Lake Worth Herald, Florida History Center & Museum, Business Development Board of Palm Beach County, Pope Theatre Company, Palm Beach Zoo at Dreher Park, Old School Square, Raymond F. Kravis Center for the Performing Arts, Palm Beach Opera, City of West Palm Beach, Sunfest Festival, "Mac" McLaughlin and Anne Hursley of the Palm Beach County Convention & Visitors Bureau. Special thanks to Jesse Newman whose direction and knowledge of the community were a cornerstone in this production. Fred Eckel and Linda Hersh proof read and gave general assistance and also deserve special thanks as does Christina Wood for her corporate sponsors biographies, and the photographers who dispatched themselves throughout the community and returned with extraordinary images. Finally, John P. Johnson of the Judge James R. Knott Center for Historic Preservation, now serving as the regional office of the Florida Division of Historic Preservation, read the entire work and made many valuable suggestions. This contribution is particularly appreciated and we thank him.

Photo C. J. Walker.

Introduction

The 2,054 square miles of land known today as Palm Beach County takes its name from a small barrier island of only six square miles in size. Many people played important roles in the history of Palm Beach and the county which bears its name. Still, no one had more influence on the development of Palm Beach, and indeed all of Florida, than Standard Oil founding partner, Henry Morrison Flagler.

The history of Palm Beach really began with the Second Seminole Indian war when United States soldiers, driving the Native Americans south down the peninsular, named the body of water separating the barrier island from Lake Worth for their general, William J. Worth. However, the first person of European descent to actually inhabit the island was probably August O. Lang, who came to the area to avoid capture by union patrol boats after he helped other Confederate sympathizers dismantle the lantern at Jupiter Lighthouse.

In the 1870s a few settlers made their way through Florida's wilderness to settle on the island and around Lake Worth. The island was eventually named, and recognized by the United States Post Office, as Palm Beach in 1887. However, until 1909 the area now known as Palm Beach County remained part of Dade County, an extremely large and sparsely populated area covering 7,200 square miles, including the whole of Lake Okeechobee to the north and extending as far south as the keys. The 1890 census shows only 726 people inhabiting this vast area, an average of only one person per ten square miles. Henry Flagler changed all of that by creating tourism and agriculture industries which even now, 100 years later, remain the mainstay of Florida's economy and Flagler's legacy.

Flagler dramatically shaped Florida's future because he realized that the state's natural beauty and climate could support tourism and agriculture if he could develop a system of transportation to bring people to the area and ship agricultural products to the rest of the nation. Flagler began building the Florida East Coast Railway system which eventually connected the entire east coast from Jacksonville to Key West. He made it possible for someone to board a train almost anywhere in the eastern United States and travel to Florida in 36 hours or less. Along the way Flagler built luxury hotels, established many cities, and promoted the agricultural development of nearly 2,000,000 acres of land. In Palm Beach County Flagler built two of his grandest and most luxurious hotels and the public works system for West Palm Beach. Of all the places Henry Flagler might of chosen to build his winter home, he chose the island of Palm Beach. And Whitehall, the gilded Cage estate Flagler built here in 1902 is open to the public as Flagler Museum.

Flagler believed the combination of the glamorous life style he initiated with his luxury hotels and the winter estate, and the natural beauty and climate of the area, would make Palm Beach one of the most popular places in the world to live and visit. Today the population of Palm Beach County tops a million; the island from which it takes its name is known the world over as a haven for the wealthy and famous, and the hundreds of millions of visitors during the last one hundred years have proven Flagler correct.

John M. Blades, Executive Director, Henry Morrison Flagler Museum.

Photo courtesy Henry Morrison Flagler Museum/Lucien Capehart.

The annual Okeechobee Cattleman's Rodeo, attracts more than 150 participants and 10,000 spectators for bareback riding, steer wrestling, barrel races, bull riding, saddle bronco riding, wild horse races, and the event The Okeechobee Rodeo is known for, calf roping. Photo The Palm Beach Post/Paul Milette.

The Early Days

By Donald W. Curl, Ph.D.

A 1909 act of the Florida legislature created Palm Beach County from the northern end of Dade County. The area had earlier been known as the Lake Country, a reference to the twenty-two-mile-long coastal lake first discovered by soldiers during the Second Seminole Indian War and named for Colonel William Jenkins Worth, the last commander of the war. With no roads in the area and sailboats providing the only form of transportation, all settlements were along the shores of the lake.

In 1853 Congress authorized the construction of a lighthouse at Jupiter Inlet, the first building in what became Palm Beach County. Extreme heat, mosquitoes,

Billy Bowlegs standing in his Florida garden. A party of army surveyors destroyed the garden in 1855, opening the short lived Third Seminole Indian War. In 1858 Bowlegs surrendered and agreed to be shipped to the west. This short war delayed the construction of the Jupiter Lighthouse. Photo Historical Society of Palm Beach County.

and sand flies made the life of the builders miserable. An Indian conflict temporarily delayed work on the lighthouse which was finally completed in July 1860, less than a year before the outbreak of the Civil War.

During the war, supporters of the South maintained that the lighthouse aided the North's naval blockade of the Florida coast. August O. Lang, the assistant keeper of the light, with the help of other Southern sympathizers, hid part of the light's mechanism. Captain James A. Armour, a former New Yorker and an ardent Union man, came to the Indian River area in the 1850s. During the war he served as volunteer pilot for the Union patrol boat *Sagamore* which caught many blockade runners attempting to supply the Confederacy from the Bahamas.

After the war Armour restored the missing parts to the light and became its assistant keeper in 1866. Three years later in 1869, he began his thirty-six-year service as head keeper at Jupiter. In the 1870s and 1880s, almost everyone going south to the lake country, including the pioneers who settled Palm Beach County, stopped at the light and many served a period as Armour's assistant keeper.

The first resident of the lake country was August Lang, the former assistant keeper who had disabled the light. Fearing arrest by the crews of the coastal patrols, he moved to the lake during the war, though settling afterwards in the Indian River area. In November 1872 an old sailor named Charles Moore became the second settler. In the next few years a number of pioneers arrived, including Hannibal D. Pierce, his wife Margaretta Moore Pierce, and their son Charles. Charles Pierce told the story of these early settlers in his book, *Pioneer Life in Southeast Florida*.

In 1876 the Dimick family of Constantine, Michigan came to the lake. Elisha "Cap" Dimick later opened its first tourist hotel, served in the state legislature, and became Palm Beach's first mayor. Like most of the early settlers, Dimick at first planned to farm. Although tropical Florida posed problems for farmers trained in more temperate climates, the rich muck and red-hammock lands proved highly productive and they soon produced bumper crops of sweet potatoes, Indian pumpkins, and pineapples. Although highly profitable, pineapple cultivation was extremely hard work. Within a few years a blight hit the fields, and then Caribbean pineapples entered the American market, reducing the profits for the domestic crop. By the 1890s, most pioneer farmers grew vegetables for the northern winter market. While they produced tomatoes, beans, eggplants, melons, and strawberries in abundance, rough seas and unfavorable wind conditions often delayed delivery and spoiled the crop. Consequently, vegetable farming remained a precarious business until the coming of the railroad.

As the number of settlers grew, they demanded regular mail service from the post office. Throughout the 1870s, the lake residents received mail only when a trustworthy traveler passed through. Finally, in May

Elisha N. "Cap" Dimick added eight rooms to his house in 1880 and opened the Cocoanut Grove House to winter tourists. He later became a state senator and then the first mayor of the town of Palm Beach. Photo Historical Society of Palm Beach County.

Colonel William Jenkins Worth, the last American commander of the army in Florida during the Second Seminole Indian War. As the soldiers shipped captured Seminoles west to reservations and drove the remaining Indians to the southern tip of the Everglades, Worth could declare the war ended on August 14, 1842. Photo Historical Society of Palm Beach County.

An Indian conflict temporarily delayed work on the Jupiter lighthouse which was finally completed in July 1860, less than a year before the outbreak of the Civil War. Photo Palm Beach County Convention & Visitors Bureau.

The Orange Grove House of Refuge # 3, located just north of Atlantic Avenue in Delray Beach. Built in 1876 as a haven for ship wreck survivors, the first keeper was Hannibal D. Pierce, whose son Charles wrote The First Account of Life in Pioneer Southeast Florida. Photo Historical Society of Palm Beach County.

1880, the government opened the Lake Worth post office on the island of Palm Beach. At the time, the name "Lake Worth" applied to the entire lake country. Also during this period the federal government came to realize the extremely isolated nature of the southeastern Florida coast. Although the Florida reef had taken a large toll of ships, the broad sandy beaches often allowed shipwreck victims to reach the shore safely. Unfortunately, once on shore, they could find no shelter, food, or water in the isolated area. To overcome this problem, the United States Life Savings Service constructed five ocean front houses of refuge, each stocked with food and water, and manned by a keeper.

In 1876 the Life Savings Service completed the Orange Grove House of Refuge at Delray Beach. It became a way station on one of the post office's most unusual routes. In 1885 it created a mail route from Lake Worth to Biscayne Bay. With no roads to Miami, the carrier walked the sixty miles down the ocean beach. As the carrier made better time walking on the wet sand near the sea, to save his shoes from the salt water, he walked barefoot. In his 1943 novel *The Barefoot Mailman*, Theodore Pratt called this the "Barefoot Route." It took the carrier six days to make the round-trip from the Lake to Miami. He kept boats in order to cross the Hillsboro and New River Inlets and one at the head of Biscayne Bay. James Edward Hamilton, a lake settler from Kentucky, became the most famous barefoot mailman. On this southbound journey in October 1887 someone took his small boat across the Hillsboro Inlet and Hamilton disappeared while trying to retrieve it.

The 1880s also witnessed the first of the well-to-do seasonal tourists who purchased property and built houses on the lake. Robert R. McCormick, a Denver businessman, built a substantial lake front cottage in

Stevan Dohanos painted a series of murals that depicted the hardships of the "Barefoot Route," certainly the most unusual mail route in postal history. The mailman walked barefoot to Miami. The murals are at the Main West Palm Beach Post Office. Photo Historical Society of Palm Beach County.

The Seminole Indian visitors to pioneer Clamatis Street seemed quite at home among the tent homes and simple framed stores. Photo Historical Society of Palm Beach County.

A "tin can tourist" from St. Louis, Missouri arrived in front of the Lake Worth Herald building in the 1920s. During the land boom days of the mid-1920s, many northerners drove to Florida to check out real estate opportunities. Many arrived in the summer when most of the hotels were closed and were forced to sleep in their "tin cans." Photo Lake Worth Herald.

This unidentified cowboy poses in his new finery at the turn of the century. Photo St. Lucie County Historical Museum.

Mother and child believed to be local pioneers in the Jupiter area. Photo The Florida History Center & Museum, Inc. Jupiter, Florida.

The Hotel Ponce de Leon in St. Augustine, Henry Flagler's first venture in developing the Florida East Coast. Flagler asked the son of his minister, Thomas Hastings, an Ecole de Beaux-Arts trained architect, to give him plans for the building in Spanish style. Hastings then formed what became one of America's most successful architectural partnerships with former classmate, John Carrere. They designed both the Ponce de Leon and Alcazar hotels in St. Augustine and Whitehall in Palm Beach. They were also the architects for the New York Public Library. Photo Henry Morrison Flagler Museum Archives.

Facing page: Henry Morrison Flagler in around 1909. The Standard Oil partner of John D. Rockefeller and Florida East Coast developer visited Palm beach in 1892 and decided to extend his railroad to the island and build a luxury hotel, creating the fashionable resort. Photo Henry Morrison Flagler Museum Archives.

1886. He was followed by Philadelphia soap maker Charles I. Cragin, C. Vanderbilt Barton of New York, Chicago mayor George B. Swift, and members of the Cluett family, the Arrow shirtmakers of Troy, New York. These wealthy northerners all built large, seasonal houses on the lake front.

Local legend claims that Henry M. Flagler extended his railroad to the Lake Worth area and built a resort hotel after he saw the luxuriously appointed McCormick cottage in Palm Beach. Flagler, a partner of John D. Rockefeller in the Standard Oil Company, both purchased the land for his hotel and the McCormick house for his own residence.

Flagler first made his mark in Florida when he built the Ponce de Leon hotel in St. Augustine. In order to move his guests to the "Ancient City" he also purchased a small narrow-gauge railroad that ran from the south bank of the Saint Johns River to Saint Augustine. With the success of the Ponce de Leon, Flagler continued to build and purchase hotels and add to his railroad mileage until he reached Daytona. Although he secured a charter from the State of Florida to build to Miami, he seemed to feel that connecting his railroad with the Indian River steamboats at either Rockledge or Melbourne would complete his southern expansion. His visit to Palm Beach in March 1892 brought both relief and happiness to the people of the lake country, and set off the area's first land boom. While buying land in Palm Beach for his hotel, he also purchased the property that became West Palm Beach. From the first, Flagler planned to make Palm Beach a resort community and build a commercial city on the western shore of the lake to care for tourists' needs.

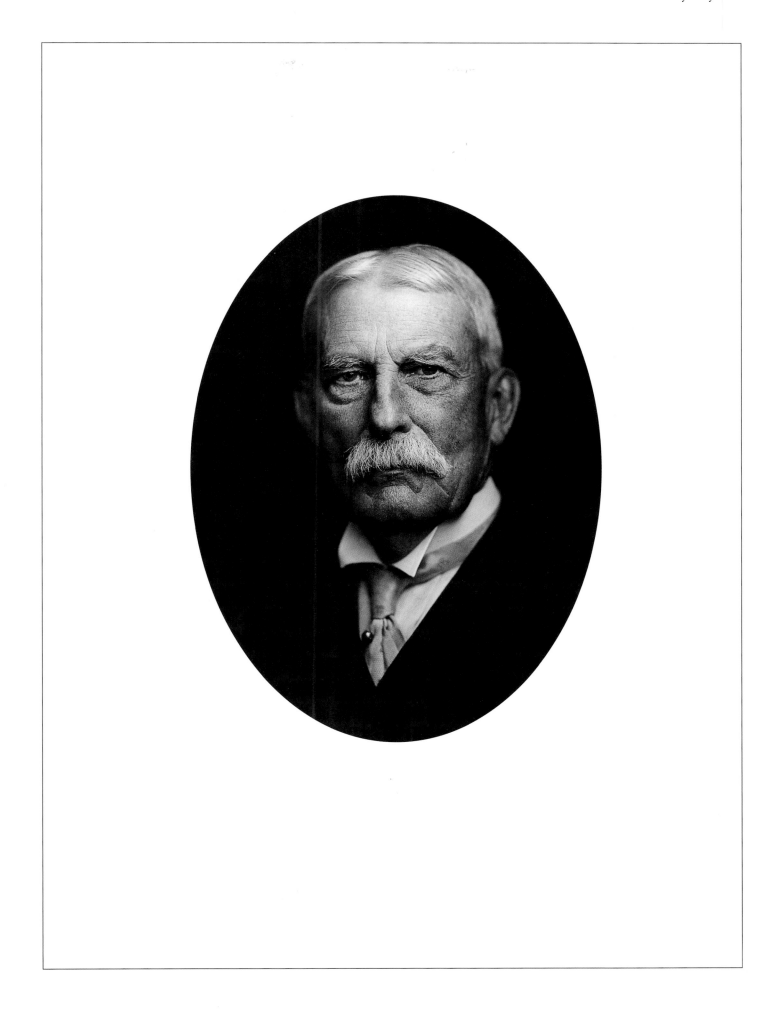

Laying tracks on the Florida East Coast Railway. Although Henry Flagler's charter from the State of Florida allowed him to build a line all the way to Miami, he at first seemed satisfied with Palm Beach as his southern terminus. When "The Great Freeze of 1895" destroyed crops in the Palm Beach region, though not around Miami, Flagler decided to build on to Biscayne Bay. Construction started in September 1895 and the first passenger train arrived on April 15, 1896. Photo Henry Morrison Flagler Museum Archives.

The Royal Poinciana Hotel opened in February 1894. Although skeptics questioned Flagler's ability to fill its original 540 rooms, the hotel proved popular from the first. In 1899 and 1901 he built large additions to the hotel which ultimately covered thirty-two acres with three miles of corridors and 1,081 rooms. In 1896 he erected the ocean front Palm Beach Inn, changing its name to the Breakers in 1900. It also proved popular and when a 1903 fire destroyed the structure he quickly constructed a larger hotel.

Although the Royal Poinciana opened in February, the first train reached West Palm Beach only on April 2, 1894. In 1895 Flagler built a bridge across Lake Worth for the railroad. The tracks crossed the lake south of the Royal Poinciana and continued across the island to the end of a steel pier where passengers could transfer to ships bound for Nassau.

During this period, tragedy entered Flagler's personal life. He had committed his second wife, Alice, to a private asylum for the insane after she declared her engagement to the tsar of Russia. In 1899 the courts declared her insane and although Flagler wanted out of the marriage, New York law failed to recognize insanity as grounds for divorce. Later that same year, Flagler became a resident of Palm Beach and his agents began lobbying Florida legislators to allow divorce in cases of incurable insanity. In 1901 the act passed, though state newspapers accused Flagler of buying the legislation and labeled it the "Flagler Divorce Law."

On August 13, 1901, Dade County granted Flagler his divorce and a week later he married Mary Lily Kenan of North Carolina. During his annual visit to Palm Beach, Flagler had continued to live in the McCormick cottage. He now ordered the construction of Whitehall, a $2.5-million, white-marble mansion on the Palm Beach lake front just south of the Royal Poinciana, as a wedding gift for his new bride. When they moved into the mansion in 1902, Mary Lily complained of the noise from the trains on the tracks just south of the house. By the beginning of the next season, Flagler had relocated the bridge and tracks to the north side of the Royal Poinciana.

From its opening on February 11, 1894, the Royal Poinciana hotel attracted the elite of American society. Shown in 1896 are Colonel Philip Lydig and Gladys Vanderbilt (sitting); Helen Morton (in veil), Amy Townsend, Mrs Cornelius Vanderbilt, and Mable Gerry; Captain A. T. Rose and Edith Bishop (heads visible only); Thomas Cushing, Edward Livingston, and Craig Wadsworth; Gertrude Vanderbilt, Lispenard Stewart, and Henry Payne Whitney. Photo Henry Morrison Flagler Museum Archives.

The Washington Birthday Ball became the final event of the short Palm Beach season during the Flagler years. In 1903 the ball was held in Whitehall's Louis XV ballroom. Although called the Bal Poudre, few guests seem to have worn powdered wigs to the lavish event. Photo Henry Morrison Flagler Museum Archives.

On March 18, 1925 the Breakers hotel burned for the second time. It signaled the end of the era of wooden hotels in southeast Florida. The third Breakers, a magnificent Italianate masonry structure, designed by the New York architects Schulze and Weaver, opened in January 1926. Photo Henry Morrison Flagler Museum Archives.

Mary Lily Kenan of Kenansville, North Carolina. When Ida Alice Shourds, Flagler's second wife, became insane, he convinced the Florida legislature to pass a law allowing insanity as grounds for divorce. After the law passed in 1901, Flagler, now a resident of Palm Beach, divorced Ida Alice and married Mary Lily who received the palatial Whitehall as her husband's wedding gift. Photo Henry Morrison Flagler Museum Archives.

Colonel Edward Riley Bradley remained one of Palm Beach's most respected citizens for almost a half century though his primary business was gambling. Both his Palm Beach casino The Beach Club, and his Idle Hour Farm in Kentucky combined respectable business with betting activities. Photo Historical Society of Palm Beach County.

Facing page top: Colonel Edward Bradley's Beach Club stood on the north side of Royal Poinciana Way & North Lake Trail from 1890 to 1945, although a gambling casino, and gambling was illegal in Florida, it was raided only once and without any arrests. Bradley contributed generously to political campaigns and local charities and churches, including Palm Beach's Saint Edward's Roman Catholic Church. Photo Historical Society of Palm Beach County.

Facing page: A fashionably attired group picnicking at the Breakers beach in the 1920s. Rules for bathers at the beach prohibited women from showing any "skin." Connie Lewis, an ex-minor league baseball player policed the beach. His famous cry when finding someone who had transgressed was, "Ladies, rules is rules." Photo Henry Morrison Flagler Museum Archives.

From the first, the Royal Poinciana and the Breakers attracted the elite of American society. Their guest lists often read like a national social register with everyone from Astors to Vanderbilts appearing for at least part of the short New Year's Day to Washington's Birthday resort season. A fashionable woman arrived with her own maids, trunks of clothing, and a safe full of jewelry. A typical day might begin with morning on the beach, followed by lunch at the hotel, afternoon sightseeing or golf, the tea dance at the Cocoanut Grove, and then dinner at the hotel or at Colonel Edward R. Bradley's Beach Club, which was noted for its excellent chef.

The Beach Club, a gambling casino located just north of the Royal Poinciana Hotel, opened in 1899 and although completely illegal in Florida, only closed in 1945, the year before Bradley's death. In this nearly half century, officials raided the club only once. Bradley was extremely generous to local charities and churches, and especially to political campaigns. Moreover, many believed a gambling casino necessary to keep the tourists coming to Palm Beach.

The resort's social life in the years before World War I centered on the Flagler hotels. Since the season remained short, few resorters built their

own houses. Those who did most often followed the example of early residents and constructed modest cottages on the lake front. They also continued to look to the hotels for their social life.

The person most responsible for creating a new Palm Beach society was Paris Singer, son of Isaac M. Singer, the sewing machine magnate. Singer had spent most of his life in Europe. He returned to the United States in 1917 after converting his estates in France and in England into hospitals to help with the Allied war effort. In New York he met Addison Mizner, a society architect with a Long Island country house practice. Singer's interest in architecture and Mizner's outgoing personality and wit had cemented an almost instant friendship and Singer invited Mizner to spend the winter season of 1918 in Palm Beach. The architect's practice had ended with the building restrictions of the war, and since he was convalescing after an injury, he immediately accepted.

Both Singer and Mizner found hotel social life boring. Singer also wished to help with the war effort. Consequently, he decided to build a convalescent hospital for victims of shell-shock that could serve in the postwar period as a private social club. After purchasing Joe's Alligator Farm, a longtime tourist attraction, Singer asked Mizner to design the clubhouse.

Mizner, from a prominent California family, spent a short time in 1889 in Guatemala where his father served as an American minister. This experience proved central to his life. He learned to speak Spanish and fell under the spell of Spanish culture and art. Later he attended lectures at the University of Salamanca in Spain, discovered the unique beauty of Spanish architecture, and determined to become an architect. On his return to San Francisco he apprenticed with famed architect Willis Polk. Mizner had then established his New York practice in 1904.

When construction started on Singer's clubhouse in the summer of 1918, Mizner could find no appropriate roof tiles, lighting fixtures, ornamental iron work, or furniture available to complete the building. His decision to establish workshops to make these materials in West Palm Beach marked the genesis of Mizner Industries, the city's largest manufacturing concern in the 1920s.

Addison Mizner (1872 - 1933) on his patio at 1800 South Ocean Boulevard, his third Palm Beach house, in 1922. Mizner built three ocean front houses, only to sell them within a few years at large profits. Finally, he built a town house next to his office on Worth Avenue. On his shoulder is his monkey Johnnie Brown. Photo Historical Society of Palm Beach County.

Unable to find appropriate roof tiles, lighting fixtures, ornamental iron work or furniture, Addison Mizner established what became the largest manufacturing concern in West Palm Beach in the 1920s. Photo John Johnson.

Owners of Palm Beach mansions who falsely claim Addison Mizner as its architect can perhaps be forgiven. His manufacturing plant, Mizner Industries, made the columns, door and window surroundings, wrought-iron grills and lanterns, and roof and floor tiles for most Palm Beach houses in the era of the 1920s. Photo Historical Society of Palm Beach County.

Although Singer sent thousands of invitations to victims of shell-shock, the end of the war and the isolation of southeast Florida, conspired to keep the building from becoming a hospital. Instead, Singer changed its name to the Everglades Club and when it opened on January 15, 1919, its wealthy and socially prominent charter members assured its status as the new center of resort social life. Before the end of the season, 300 additional members had joined.

After the war many resorters decided to build Palm Beach houses. The Everglades Club, with it's highly romantic and yet completely practical architecture for the southeastern Florida climate, captured the attention of the "Grande dame of the winter set," Eva Stotesbury, wife of senior J.P. Morgan partner Edward Stotesbury, who had decided to build the first great Palm Beach villa since Flagler's Whitehall. A Philadelphia architect had completed plans for a Beaux Arts-style mansion for her ocean front estate. However, after Eva Stotesbury saw the Everglades Club, she asked Mizner to prepare new plans.

El Mirasol, the house Mizner designed for the Stotesburys, embodied the techniques he used in dozens of different villas. He placed the main rooms on the beach ridge, overlooking the sea. The entrance, to the side and often on a lower level, allowed guests a dramatic entry up a broad staircase. Open loggias and cloisters surrounded a patio on the west and protected the doors and windows from the sun. All of the major rooms opened onto the loggias and terraces, allowing residents and guests easy access to the outdoors. His rambling tile roofs, lofty towers, elegantly detailed yet restrained decoration, and richly paneled and beamed rooms, created an architecture that seemed completely at home in tropical America.

El Mirasol confirmed Eva's status as society queen and made Mizner the resort's most fashionable architect. Harold Vanderbilt, the Munn brothers, Anthony J. Drexel Biddle, Angier B. Duke, Edward Shearson, Rodman Wanamaker, and Henry C. Phipps all commissioned villas in the next few years. In 1923 alone Mizner had seventeen major projects.

Over the years, Florida always seemed to produce an excess of promoters. Beginning with Everglades drainage in the 1880s through Flagler's attempts to sell the acreage his railway acquired from state grants, someone was always huckstering a piece of land. The mild winter climate that had drawn visitors to Florida for years, the post war prosperity, the automobile and improved road systems, and the profits that early investors had made in real estate transactions, all came together to produce a new land boom in the first half of the 1920s.

All of Palm Beach County shared in the speculative fever. From Harry S. Kelsey's Kelsey City (today's Lake Park) to Addison Mizner's "new" Boca Raton, developments sprang up across the county. While they all promised the finest of amenities, more to the point, they also promised constantly rising land values and assured the early buyer a tidy profit in the shortest possible time.

Tea time on the marble patio at the Everglades Club. Originally the patio contained a small grove of trees and was known as the Orange Court, when the club opened in 1919 there were no oranges on the trees, Mizner, always careful of details, purchased oranges and attached them to the trees with hair pins. Photo Historical Society of Palm Beach County.

Ned Stotesbury's birthday party on February 26, came to rival the Washington Birthday Ball as the highlight of the Palm Beach "season." The guest list grew larger each year, reaching 1,200 people by the mid - 1930s. Stotesbury always played the drum, recalling his Civil War service as a drummer boy, and sang "The Old Family Toothbrush That Hung by the Sink." Photo Historical Society of Palm Beach County.

El Mirasol, winter residence of Eva Cromwell and Edward Townsend Stotesbury. Completed in 1919, it was architect Addison Mizner's first great ocean front mansion in Palm Beach and created the style for the town in the 1920s. Photo Historical Society of Palm Beach County.

Eva Cromwell Stotesbury had already earned the title of GRAND DAME of Palm Beach society when she commissioned Addison Mizner to design her grand ocean front mansion El Mirasol. Photo Historical Society of Palm Beach County.

Land booms, like those in the stock market, depend upon confidence. The land speculator needs assurances that the value of land will rise, and that a buyer will always be available. Florida newspapers often published stories of land trading hands several times in just a few days and doubling in price each time. Publicity from the various promotions emphasized the prominent people who had invested in the enterprise. Mizner's Boca Raton claimed T. Coleman du Pont as its chairman and Harold and William K. Vanderbilt, Rodman Wanamaker, Irving Berlin, and Elizabeth Arden among its investors.

The peak of the boom came during the 1925 season when buyers snapped up any land offered, selling out new developments within hours. Problems for the boom surfaced during the summer. With so many involved in selling real estate or in the construction business, no one was available for basic service work. This resulted in hundreds of railroad freight cars left unloaded in south Florida rail yards. With so many cars entering Florida and so few leaving, the railroads decided on an embargo of all except perishable goods. This halted many construction projects, which in turn, left the impression of a troubled boom. Moreover, during the summer many people who had never visited Florida decided to drive down the Dixie Highway with their families for a summer holiday. When they arrived they found hotels and restaurants closed for the season, stores without fresh vegetables, a shortage of ice, and heat, humidity, and mosquitoes. On returning home they told everyone about how terrible life could be in Florida.

During this same period, northern banks, seeing money supplies drained off for Florida land purchases, began a campaign to warn potential investors about the hazards of the boom. All of these problems helped shake the confidence of the buyers. Although Florida real estate interests claimed that people "bought to live in Florida," most buyers knew they made land purchases for a quick profit. At the first sign of trouble, many sold immediately. With its well-known backers, Mizner's Boca Raton development seemed one of the safest investments. When sales faltered, the company added more promises to its claims about the city. Fearful that they might be held to these claims, du Pont and some of the other backers resigned from the board and published a letter in the *New York Times* in which they denied financial responsibility for fulfilling the company promises.

Although Mizner completed the small Cloister Inn that later grew into the Boca Raton Resort and Club, and several other Boca Raton projects, the boom had collapsed by the summer of 1926. When the September 1926 hurricane hit south Florida with its massive destruction, the buyers had already disappeared.

Developers in Palm Beach County and across Florida found themselves forced into bankruptcy. In most cases their towns and suburbs languished until after World War II. Boca Raton found a savior in Clarence

SEABOARD STATION RESTORATION FOUNDATION, INC.

SEABOARD RAILWAY STATION · 192

OLIVER GLIDDEN & PARTNERS ARCHITECTS & PLANNER

M. Tammany, del.

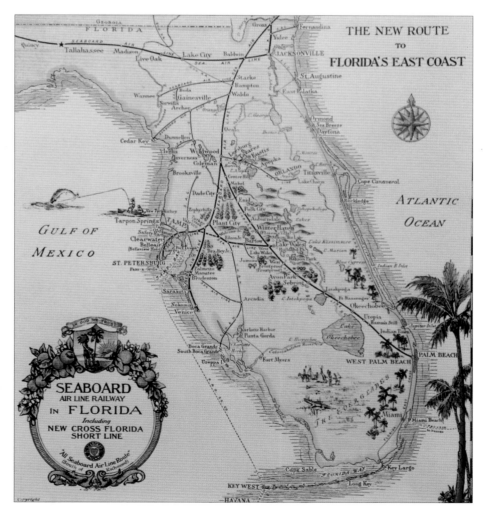

THE NEW ROUTE
TO
FLORIDA'S EAST COAST

SEABOARD
AIR LINE RAILWAY
IN FLORIDA
Including
NEW CROSS FLORIDA
SHORT LINE

The Seaboard Air Line Railroad Station in West Palm Beach. Designed by Harvey and Clarke, the station was recently restored and remains one of Tri Rails most elegant stations. Photo Historical Society of Palm Beach County.

In January 1925, S. Davis Warfield's Seaboard Air Line Railroad began regular service to West Palm Beach. This second railroad challenged the Florida East Coast Railway's hold on southeast Florida. Warfield's niece, Wallis, often visited Palm Beach after she became the Duchess of Windsor. Photo John Johnson.

The West Palm Beach Station opened with the arrival of the Orange Blossom Special in January 1925. Post card John Johnson.

Geist, an original investor in Mizner's company. He purchased the Mizner interests, built a large addition to the hotel, and opened it as the Boca Raton Club.

The end of the boom marked the beginning of a depression for Florida and for most residents of Palm Beach County. The rapid expansion in every area that came with the boom had forced the county's towns to issue bonds to pay for water purification and sewage treatment plants, new streets, recreational facilities, and new city halls to house the added employees needed to service the growing population. The new private construction and the rising value of real estate saw a corresponding rise in property tax collections which city fathers believed guaranteed the payment of the bonds.

When the boom ended, the bottom fell out of property values. Banks failed across the county. Depositors lost their savings. Businesses failed and employees lost their jobs. And then in 1928 a second major hurricane hit landfall at Palm Beach and swept westward across the county leaving devastation and death in its wake. Almost every town in the county felt the economic depression at least two years before the collapse of the New York stock market.

Palm Beach County only began to recover from the lingering problems of depression when the Army Air Corps established bases in West Palm Beach and Boca Raton during World War II. West Palm Beach's Morrison Field processed aircraft and air personnel for overseas duty. In the period before the Normandy invasion, over 6,000 airplanes and 45,000 personnel passed through the field on the way to Europe. Later, wounded servicemen returned to the states through West Palm Beach and the Breakers Hotel became Ream Army Hospital, noted for its occupational therapy division.

The base in Boca Raton trained airmen in the use of radar. As the country's only radar school, as many as 40,000 men passed through its courses. The army constructed over 800 buildings on the base and even took over the Boca Raton Club to house officers. The base completely overwhelmed the little town and its civilian work force came from as far away as Fort Lauderdale. At the end of the war the radar training school moved to Mississippi and the air field later became home to Florida Atlantic University. The West Palm Beach field became Palm Beach International Airport.

During the war years, thousands of young men had served at various bases in south Florida. The memory of balmy winter days with crystal clear sunny skies proved a strong attraction and many returned. Although summer's heat and humidity remained, fortunately, air conditioning had became an everyday reality. The result saw the beginning of a new land boom, though one with a sounder economic basis. Many middle-and upper-income retirees, sought the good life in Palm Beach County and new subdivisions and cities catered to their visions. New industries also helped

support the growing population. Industrial giants like Pratt-Whitney and IBM established Palm Beach County plants as did many smaller concerns.

In the years after World War II, John D. MacArthur and Arthur Vining Davis made major contributions to Palm Beach County. Like Flagler both men had made fortunes before they came to Florida, and like Flagler they used their fortunes, in what should have been their retirement, to build new empires. MacArthur's close to three billion dollar fortune came from Bankers Life, a Chicago insurance company. Davis made his fortune in the Aluminum Corporation of America (Alcoa).

MacArthur's land empire started in the 1950s when he foreclosed on a large loan made to a developer. By 1976 *Newsweek* magazine claimed that he owned 100,000 acres, much in Palm Beach County, which made him Florida's largest landowner. In the next few years he developed Lake Park, North Palm Beach, and Palm Beach Gardens, which became his major project. He brought a $4-million RCA factory to Palm Beach Gardens in 1962 and in 1964 he built golf courses and a clubhouse for the Professional Golfers Association. Although one of the nation's wealthiest men, he cultivated a casual style, dressing in baggy sweaters, rolling his own cigarettes, driving an old car, and directing operations of his insurance and development businesses from a Formica-topped table in a corner of his hotel's coffee shop.

MacArthur always claimed to be opposed to charity. Nonetheless, when he died in 1978 he placed his immense fortune of almost $3 billion in the John D. and Catherine T. MacArthur Foundation. The foundation has given millions to many causes and has shown its generosity to Palm Beach County. Its real estate division has preserved thousands of acres on the headwaters of the Loxahatchee River and gave the land for the 288-acre John D. MacArthur State Park.

While MacArthur bought land in the northern part of the county, Davis, who cut his ties with Alcoa and moved to his Miami retirement home, became the south county tycoon. In 1956 he purchased the Boca Raton Hotel and Club and 1,500 acres of land from J. Myer Schine for $22.5 million. Schine, who owned a chain of theatres and hotels, had purchased the hotel in 1944 for $2.5 million. By 1958, Davis owned 140,000 acres in south Florida and the Bahamas. In that year he turned 91 and realized the need to bring order to these holdings. Consequently, he formed the Arvida Corporation (the first two letters of his names) which became one of the major real estate developers in south Florida. Before his death in 1962 the company had started University Park and the ritzy Royal Palm Yacht and Country Club in Boca Raton.

In 1966, just two years after Florida Atlantic University opened in Boca Raton, Arvida sold 550 acres of land to IBM. The company said they chose the location because of climate, orange juice, the university, and the airport. When IBM decided to launch a desk-top computer for home and business use in 1980, a team headed by Philip "Don" Estridge at the Boca

Raton plant took just eighteen months to develop the personal computer, or PC. The PC's sales skyrocketed and soon IBM employed 9,500 people at the local facility. Although later IBM transferred its development and manufacturing processes to other areas, the gigantic Marcel Breuer-designed plant remains, today the home to a number of smaller companies and the United States Post Office.

Palm Beach County continued its expansion and development throughout the 1980s and into the 1990s, mimicking economic trends of the nation. By the turn of the century it is estimated that the county's population will be more than a million. Today, Palm Beach County is the northern most point of that long coastal metropolitan area that stretches from southern Dade County, through all of Broward, and ends near the northern Palm Beach County line. The nearly 5 million people who live in the three counties make it one of the nation's largest metropolitan areas.

PGA National Golf Club offers 5 championship courses to resident members and resort visitors. Photo PGA National.

The Riches of The Land

By Thomas J. Schueneman, Ph.D.

A billion dollar agriculture county? It's true! Palm Beach County is internationally renown for its agricultural production.

The county is the largest in area of Florida's 67 counties. Originally carved out of Dade County, it stretches from the Atlantic Ocean on the east to more than half way around Lake Okeechobee to the west, and covers 2,023 square miles of land and 245 square miles of water. Of this land area, only 900 square miles is farmed. Yet, agricultural land is in danger of extinction. When we look at the population explosion in the county, the number of people making this their retirement home, and the lure of our sunshine and beautiful beaches, it is

An unlikely facet of Palm Beach County's diversity can be witnessed in its agricultural industry. The rich bounty of the land has made the county a leader in agricultural production. With technological advancements this sun drenched haven is keeping pace with the demand for land development. Photo The Palm Beach Post/Greg Lovett.

easy to understand the developmental pressures facing agricultural land. Why is agriculture so important to Palm Beach County? This one industry has yearly sales of over one billion dollars, provides over 20,000 jobs, and accounts for an economic impact of nearly three billion dollars a year.

Blessed with abundant sunshine, water, and arable land, the county has evolved into a national leader in the production of sugar cane, peppers, sweet corn, radishes, and Chinese vegetables. It is also important in the production of nursery and foliage plants, sod, tomatoes, celery, lettuce crops, citrus, rice, and horses. During the 1987-88 production year, wholesale value of these products surpassed the billion dollar mark and has continued to climb.

Estimated Palm Beach County Crop Values in 1996

Sugarcane–$600 million, Vegetables–$200 million, Ornamentals–$150 million, Sod–$46 million, Horses–$42 million, Citrus–$19 million, Rice–$12 million.

The history of agriculture in Palm Beach County is characterized by a pioneering spirit normally associated with the settlers of the Great Plains. Early coastal settlers arrived first by sailboat, then by steamer, and later by train. Palmetto swamps, pine forests, and sandy soils greeted these hardy pioneers and limited early agriculture ventures to cattle and small gardens. It is said to have taken a man two months to clear one acre. In 1879, coastal settlers planted thousands of pineapple slips. Although pineapple growing proved hard work, it remained the single most important cash crop until late in the century. By the 1890s, most coastal farmers grew vegetables for the northern winter market. In the earliest days, cattle roamed free. When, and if, rounded up, cattle from these unimproved "farms" were truly wild animals.

Forty miles of swamp, forests, snakes, and alligators separated these east coast settlers from their county cousins on the shore of Lake Okeechobee. Early residents of the western edge of the county were pri-

Workers at the USDA Breeding Station in Canal Point are preparing the 1947 sugarcane seedling nursery. Later that year, flood waters covered the area for several months. Photo USDA file.

Three closely-spaced storms in the fall of 1947 caused extensive flooding over most of southeast Florida. USDA Sugarcane Research Station workers are seen returning to their cabins at Canal Point by boat. Photo USDA file.

marily fishermen and hunters. They clung to a thin sliver of elevated land sandwiched between the lake and the seemingly endless sawgrass swamp. Swarms of mosquitoes and horse flies attacked exposed flesh. Mosquitoes were so plentiful that they occasionally killed cattle by suffocation.

These hardy Lake Okeechobee pioneers were impressed with the black, seemingly fertile soils. Many had been convinced by land speculators that any crop planted there would grow. Within months of arriving, however, many left the area, discouraged by the poor crops and continuous battles with insects and water. Many believed that only native custard apple trees and some types of grass would grow, while the vegetables and cattle died.

Within ten months of entering the Union in 1845, the Florida legislature passed a resolution calling for the reclaiming of the Everglades. Numerous pieces of both state and federal legislation concerning these "swamp and overflowed lands" were enacted during the ensuing years, with the intent of making these areas suitable for habitation and cultivation. However, the slow and inadequate early efforts at drainage resulted in no significant settling in the Glades prior to 1910.

Dot Tucker, who still lives on the lake, remembers these early times well. Her father, Duke Tucker, with his father, Morgan Tucker, began fishing Lake Okeechobee in 1911, making the journey from Fort Myers via the Caloosahatchee River. In 1913 they took up permanent residence on the east shore of the lake near what is now Canal Point. Transportation at that time was by boat or mule, and neighbors were few.

Duke Tucker met a local girl, Ruby Burt. For a marriage license they had to register at the county seat, almost inaccessible in West Palm Beach. So they waited. Finally, the West Palm Beach Canal connecting West Palm Beach to the expanding town of Canal Point was completed in 1917. The next day, they made the trip to West Palm Beach to get married. That trip, traveling through forty miles of swampy savannah's and palmetto wetlands,

Ruby Burt Tucker was a pioneer in the "Glades" area. This circa 1925 picture shows her standing near the railroad trestle in Canal Point wearing her favorite beaded dress. Photo Dot Tucker.

on a barge pulled by mules or pushed along using poles, beset by heat, insects, and thunderstorms, was not for light hearted travelers. Prior to the canal's opening, all supplies to Lake Okeechobee made the dangerous seventy mile barge trip from either Fort Lauderdale or Fort Myers. Completion of the West Palm Beach Canal spurred the settling of the area. By 1921, 2,000 people lived in sixteen settlements on or near the lake.

The canal remained the only link to West Palm Beach until July 4, 1924, when the Connors Toll Highway (now US 98) opened. This road, built alongside the canal, used canal dredgings for its base. Dot Tucker, born just after the road opened, remembers that her family continued to fish until 1928 when string-bean farming finally became profitable.

Two major obstacles hampered early farming operations: lack of water control and poor soil fertility. The water control problems ranged from sporadic periods of drought to times of excessive rainfall. Droughts caused both crop losses and wild fires, some of which smoldered for months. Floods often became life threatening as exemplified by the hurricanes of 1926 and 1928, and the floods of 1922 and 1947. Even under normal conditions, farming remained a gamble, threatened by losses of crops and live-stock to the water.

Palm Beach County soils are either white sand or black muck. Sand soils, subject to the leaching effect of heavy rains for thousands of years, are nearly devoid of nutrients. Soils high in organic matter are called muck. Although a product of the same period as the white sand, muck formed in the swamp bogs that covered most of the western half of the county and were only drained in the late nineteenth and early twentieth centuries. In general, although these soils have ample nitrogen and moderate phosphorous, they have almost nothing else. Without fertilizer, sand and muck are suitable only for grass production. This lack of nutrients, especially trace elements, in all of the county's soils resulted in poor crops and unhealthy cattle.

Crop spraying with fertilizer has enabled the muck and sand soil to support thriving crops. Photo Tony Arruza.

Right: As part of the grass family, sugar cane was one of the few healthy crops first pioneered in the muck. Today over 360,000 acres are planted in sugar by over 100 individual farmers. Photo Tony Arruza.

Facing page: A Snowy Egret serenly reflects over the devestation of flooded crops. Photo Tony Arruza.

The ritual burning of sugar cane cleanses the land for the next crop. Photo The Palm Beach Post/Lannis Waters.

Facing page: The golden Florida sun sets over a field of flowering sugar cane. Photo Tony Arruza.

Sugar Cane: Since sugar cane is a grass, it could grow on low fertility muck soils. A partnership that eventually became United States Sugar Corporation harvested the first commercial sugar cane in 1919. Harvests produced 745 tons of raw sugar in 1928, increasing to 65,100 tons by 1938. In response to the growing importance of sugar cane production in both Louisiana and Florida, the United States Department of Agriculture established a sugar cane variety development station at Canal Point in 1921. While this proved an important impetus for the expansion of the Florida sugar cane industry, USDA also enacted policies that restricted growth by establishing quotas for sugar cane. As a result, the pre-1960 Florida sugar cane industry never exceeded 60,000 acres.

Triggered by the United States trade embargo against Cuba in the early 1960s and the subsequent lifting of production quotas, sugar cane acreage increased by 600%. All cattle ranches and some vegetable farms were eventually converted to sugar cane. It is now planted on 360,000 acres by over 100 individual farmers. Leaders in the industry are Flo-Sun Corporation, owned by the Fanjul family, United States Sugar Corporation, Sugar Cane Growers Cooperative of Florida, Talisman Sugar Corporation, A. Duda and Sons, and King Ranch of Florida. Sugar cane is a large, sweet grass which, in order to produce a marketable crop of sugar crystals, requires processing by a mill. Twenty-five percent of the United States sugar production comes from south Florida. Of the seven cane

A formidable mountain of raw sugar. Sugar cane is considered a forgiving crop well suited to the low fertility muck soils environmental climate of Palm Beach County. South Florida produces over 25% of America's sugar. The vast quantities of sugar cultivated in Palm Beach County have eliminated cattle ranches and some vegetable farms.. Photo Tony Arruza.

mills in Florida, six are located in western Palm Beach County.

Farmers are characterized as gamblers and a gamble that paid off is the Sugar Cane Growers Cooperative of Florida. Fifty-four growers banded together in 1960 to establish a cooperative to harvest, mill, and market their sugar. Now with 56 members and 68,000 acres, they are a major economic and political force in the county. George Wedgeworth has been the president of the Cooperative since its founding.

Flo-Sun Sugar is still playing out another gamble. Flo-Sun constructed two renewable energy biomass power plants at its Okeelanta and

Osceola sugar mills. These plants use urban wood-waste and sugar fiber, called bagasse, to produce enough electricity and steam to power the sugar mills and light over 80,000 houses. Flo-Sun Sugar, under the Florida Crystals brand name, markets nationally its own line of natural sugar and rice products. In February 1997, Florida Crystals milled the first certified organic sugar ever produced in the United States.

The future of sugar cane remains promising. Characterized as a "forgiving" crop that tolerates most of the adverse weather that periodically invades south Florida, it is truly a crop suited to our environment.

Right: Stephen Shuler Nie proudly displays a Napa type of Chinese cabbage from the Yee Farm in Boynton Beach. Photo K. D. Shuler.

Vegetables: The turning point for vegetable production occurred in the mid 1920s. An experiment by the University of Florida's Research Station established in 1921 east of Belle Glade accidentally discovered that the local soils needed trace nutrients to be productive.

Researchers used copper sulfate and lime, a concoction known as bordeaux, to control bean plant diseases. The bordeaux both controlled diseases and made the plants thrive, producing for the first time marketable beans. Quickly adopting the practice of applying copper sulfate as a fertilizer, farmers made the muck soils productive. As yields increased, researchers found the muck also needed other elements such as zinc, manganese, and boron which farmers began adding to the soil.

Railroads proved a valuable asset to early vegetable production. In 1924, Glades growers shipped 1,200 rail car loads of vegetables to points north. However, moving large amounts of produce to the rail heads remained difficult. Roads were often impassable and crops perished before reaching the railroad. The period from 1935 to 1939 saw a depressed Florida vegetable industry. Then, with the advent of World War II and the need for large quantities of fresh produce, times changed. Celery production doubled, lettuce tripled, and acreage of green beans multiplied 75 times.

Can you imagine that four out of every five radishes consumed in the nation during some of the winter months comes from Palm Beach County? The same is true for sweet corn. During the 1970s and 1980s South Bay Growers, a diversified vegetable grower and shipper located in South Bay, became the largest producer in the county. Established after World War II by C. A. "Mutt" Thomas and Billy Rogers, it expanded into celery, sweet corn, cabbage, and eventually lettuce, until yearly sales exceeded $35 million. Sold to United States Sugar Corporation in 1980, South Bay Growers continued as the largest vegetable producer in the Glades until 1994.

The importance of vegetable production peaked in 1992 with an estimated wholesale value of over $275 million. DuBois, Mecca, Pero, Thomas, Whitworth, Wing Chong, and Yee are farm names that bring to mind vast acreage of tomatoes, peppers, cucumbers, eggplant, and Chinese vegetables along the Atlantic seaboard. Sweet corn, celery, radish, lettuce items, and snapbeans are the main Everglades vegetables. Lower demand for Florida produce signaled another change: from vegetables to sugar cane in the Glades, and from vegetables to subdivisions along the coast. However, even with these latest pressures, vegetable production continues to be important for the county economy, accounting for over $200 million in gross income in 1996.

Lettuce packing like many other agricultural endeavors demands a strenuous labor pool. Photo The Palm Beach Post/Loren Hosack.

The harvesting of winter vegetable for shipment is a lucrative market. Photo Tony Arruza.

Cattle on an early misty Florida morning.
Photo The Palm Beach Post/Loren Hosack.

Cattle: The rise and fall of the cattle industry in Palm Beach County happened relatively recently. Although copper deficiency had been identified in the mid-1920s as the limiting factor for crop production on muck lands, it took another ten years to associate that same deficiency with weak and dying cattle.

The palmetto swamps that covered the eastern half of the county had been used for pastures since the late 1800s. However, they could support relatively few cattle. The growth of cattle ranching came as an indirect result of the growth of the vegetable industry. With the tremendous vegetable acreage expansion triggered by World War II, farmers found themselves usually limited to three years of good yields on a piece of land. Soil-borne diseases quickly built to levels forcing them to find fresh land. In return for the use of a neighbor's unimproved, almost worthless native pastures, the vegetable grower drained and cleared the land and then leveled and fertilized the soil. After three years of tomato or other vegetable crops, he seeded the farm back to grass and returned it to the cattle rancher as improved pasture. In this way, much of the eastern portion of the county became an important center for dairy and beef cattle production.

Two things changed this picture along the coast. First, virgin land suitable for vegetable production became scarce and expensive. Second, with the advent of relatively inexpensive soil fumigants that controlled soil-borne pathogens, it became more economical for the vegetable farmers to buy land and stay put. Consequently, between the expansion of the vegetable farms, and urban sprawl, cattle and dairy farming almost disappeared. The last dairy herd was sold about 1995.

Cattle ranching developed around Lake Okeeckobee in a different manner, though with the same eventual results. Although researchers had long known that dietary selenium improved the health of cattle grown in the Glades, the resulting quality still remained poor. Only in 1938 with the discovery that copper added to their diet resulted in healthy cattle, was there a renewed interest in raising cattle. In addition, the 1941 opening of the Thomas E. Will Highway (US 27) from South Bay to Miami signaled the expansion of the cattle industry into the vast swamps south and east of Lake Okeechobee. Local vegetable and sugar cane growers as well as out-of-state entrepreneurs cleared the swamps and established large herds. The Glades Auction Market, which held its first sale in 1950, soon became the leading livestock market in the state.

An example of one such entrepreneur is Walter Beinecke of the S & H Green Stamp fortune. He acquired 42,000 marsh acres south of Belle Glade with the intent of raising sugar cane. Because the government refused him permits for that amount of sugar cane, he turned to cattle. Joining forces with Robert J. Kleberg, Jr., president of King Ranch in Texas, the two established the Big B Ranch in November 1964.

To operate a ranch the size of Big B necessitated the digging of 257 miles of field ditches, 42 miles of lateral canals, and 40 miles of major canals. Drainage pumps with the capacity of over one million gallons per minute were installed to remove storm waters. In addition, 148 miles of rock road were built to provide access to every 80 acre tract. By 1969, practically all of the acreage was in improved grass. The ranch became famous for its pure bred Santa Gertrudis cattle.

But fame is fleeting. While King Ranch secured total ownership of Big B in 1971, the following years saw a lengthy depression in the cattle market. By 1983 King Ranch of Florida had moved completely out of the cattle business, converting most of its land to sugar cane and sod production. Currently, it is among industry leaders in both of these areas.

Santa Gertrudis cattle on Big B Ranch south of South Bay. In less than 20 years, Palm Beach County had risen from a minor player to a major force in the Florida cattle industry. Photo C King Ranch, Inc., Kingsville, Texas. (Used by permission.)

Top: A brilliant array of annuals and perennials greet the high value market daily. Photo The Palm Beach Post/Loren Hosack.

The construction boom along the Atlantic seaboard fuels a strong demand for St. Augustine Grass. Photo T. J. Schueneman.

Facing page: The equine industry represents a $230 million per year economy in Palm Beach County. Polo and horse farms cover a vast acreage. Photo C. J. Walker.

Ornamentals and Sod: Palm Beach County is nationally recognized as a leader in potted annual and perennial plants. Mild weather on the county level, urban development on a regional level, and increased consumer demand on the national level, have fueled the expansion of tree and potted plant nurseries to over 7,000 acres county-wide. In urban areas, where escalating land values have driven out conventional agriculture, high value ornamental crops still can compete. Aggressive marketing has resulted in wholesale receipts exceeding $150 million per year.

With the boom in urban development came a market for sod (ready-to-lay turf grasses). Converting 20,000 acres of sugar cane and vegetable land to Saint Augustine grass helped meet this demand. The sod market is characterized by cyclic highs and lows since demand fluctuates with the rise and fall of the new housing market. Currently, over $45 million per year of sod, mostly Saint Augustine grass, is produced.

Horses: While horses are often seen in rural areas, county residents and visitors often overlook the size of the equine industry. Polo and race horse farms cover extensive acreage in both the south county area and in Wellington. Pleasure riding is very popular and the Sheriff's Department still maintains a mounted posse. The value of the horse industry to the Palm Beach County economy is estimated at over $230 million per year.

Citrus: Citrus production still maintains a foothold with $19 million in annual sales. Most of the county's citrus is purchased for frozen concentrate, a fairly unstable market. Since all county groves are located within the Indian River Citrus Marketing District, they may use the Indian River logo as a marketing tool. While direct to the public sales increases production and handling costs, potential profits are greater. Blood's Hammock Groves and Callery-Judge Groves are leaders in direct-to-consumer marketing.

Rice: With high value crops the norm, rice is an anomaly. Land costs normally prevent low value crops such as rice from being grown in Palm Beach County. When grown in rotation with sugarcane or vegetables, the cultural and soil conservation attributes of rice far outshine its monetary return. Crops following rice produce about 20% more than without rice because soil conditions are improved, plant diseases are reduced, and root-harming insects are eliminated. The flooded rice fields are a haven for birds. And, the rice produced is renowned for its high quality. Most of the area's $11 million crop is milled by the Sem-Chi rice mill in Loxahatchee. Sem-Chi rices, which include brown, organic, and aromatic varieties, are marketed nationally in the natural foods industry.

The Future: As the theme of this chapter is meant to suggest, "urban" has replaced "agriculture" as the primary regional focus, both politically and economically. Urbanization is winning the battle for resources all along the Atlantic seaboard. Nonetheless, agriculture is still an important economic force in the western two-thirds of the county and Palm Beach will continue to rank among the nation's top five agricultural counties.

Citrus packing is "state-of-the-art" at the new Callery-Judge Grove plant at Loxahatchee. The grove and packing house are open for tours. Photo H. Callery.

PICKING ORANGES IN FLORIDA 130

A post card depicting the heyday of orange groves and orange pickers. Post card John Johnson.

Left: Rice, being a subtropical plant, is ideally suited to Palm Beach County's abundant rainfall and warm temperatures. Photo T. J. Schueneman.

Business Finance And Trade

By M. M. Cloutier

Build it and they will come. The "it" was the most fashionable winter resort in the country. "They" were the nation's financial and social elite, swarming at the turn of the century into what had been a wild and swampy frontier with a handful of pioneers. Unfortunately, greed and speculation soon derailed the carefully planned early economic development in Palm Beach County and might have sealed its economic doom. Then two unforeseen circumstances, a world war and a restored economic momentum following the war, paved a path toward progress. To the delight of development proponents and the chagrin of environmentalists, several decades of strong economic expan-

To the delight of development proponents and the chagrin of environmentalists, several decades of strong economic expansion has led to one of the fastest growing metropolitan areas in the country, breeding ever-healthier business, financial, and international trade sectors. On the heels of tourists and hundreds of new annual residents has come big business. Photo C. J. Walker.

sion has led to one of the fastest growing metropolitan areas in the country, breeding ever-healthier business, financial, and international trade sectors. On the heels of the tourists and hundreds of new annual residents has come big business with an increasingly global reach.

The genesis of that metamorphosis only substantially materialized in the 1950s. Before that, Palm Beach County focused its economy on agriculture, tourism, and the service industries and their supporting infrastructure. But even when development first took place in the area in the late 1890s, local commerce was envisioned. Henry Flagler, the Standard Oil tycoon who extended his railroad into South Florida in 1894 and carved out a winter vacation land on the island of Palm Beach, also laid the groundwork for West Palm Beach. On a swath of land between Clear Lake and Lake Worth, his surveyors laid a grid pattern of streets and built an infrastructure comprised of a water plant, an electric generator, and eventually a telephone switchboard. While Palm Beach hotel guests, like the Vanderbilts, the Astors, and the Stotesburys, enjoyed sunny leisure, a community of 564 people to the west developed a commercial economy of small business — general stores, hat and shoe makers, banks, and even saloons.

As Palm Beach resort life gained renown in the north, more people came. By the end of World War I, the advent of the automobile and a network of roads known as Dixie Highway, made the area even more accessible. Before long developers swooped down on the area, buying huge tracts of land which they subdivided and then sold at a substantial profit. A robust real estate market took off, cresting during the land boom of 1924 and 1925. Speculators feverishly bought and sold, hoping to score big. Investors announced residential and commercial real estate ventures, including Palm Beach society architect Addison Mizner's 16,000-acre mixed-use development in Boca Raton — a virtual Spanish-style city. At the time, Mizner Industries, which included the architect's professional office, antiques shops, furniture workshops, and building materials factories, was the county's largest business.

Some of the hastily announced real estate developments throughout the county materialized and helped launch today's municipalities, such as Harry Seymour Kelsey's Kelsey City, which became Lake Park. Others never did — despite the fact many people had reserved parcels. As the boom reached a pitch, property values artificially doubled, then tripled. In West Palm Beach alone, property value between 1920 and 1925 increased from $13.6 million to $61 million. As the speculative fever mounted, northern bankers, investors, and chambers of commerce retaliated with negative campaigns. The bad publicity, coupled with continually rising prices, brought doubts about investments in Florida land and made buyers wary. By the summer of 1926, the boom had busted. Then nature added further blows with killer autumn hurricanes in 1926 and 1928. The real estate industry collapsed, architectural offices, construction firms, and

building supply companies declared bankruptcy, and Mizner himself soon died in debt. When the Depression hit, a total of eleven banks folded in the county. Only Palm Beach and Boca Raton continued to develop, though under the aegis of less speculative projects.

Throughout the good and bad times of the 1920s, however, several permanent gains were made. Massive construction led to the continued commercial development of West Palm Beach, the county seat, with dozens of new downtown buildings, many of which still stand today, such as the ten-story Comeau and the fifteen-story Harvey building. A base of some 1,500 businesses had been established. Conners Highway opened the first land link with the pioneer settlements on the western side of the county. Soon farming around Lake Okeechobee emerged as a key county industry. These years also saw the establishment of the Port of Palm Beach, with regular steamship service beginning in 1925. The 1920s also saw the incorporation of over a dozen small towns so that by 1930 more than 51,000 people lived in the county.

World War II restored economic prosperity to the area. The United States Army, viewing Florida as a strategic asset due to its geography and climate, established key air bases in the county at West Palm Beach and Boca Raton where small airports had opened in the 1930s. These bases revived the depressed construction industry — and not just temporarily. During the war, tens of thousands of troops were stationed at the air bases and at hotels that had been turned into barracks or hospitals. At the end of the war, many of them returned to "paradise" or would later retire to it. By 1950, Palm Beach County's population had grown to 115,000, requiring plenty of housing, services, and infrastructure improvements. These years saw the opening of the Beeline Highway, construction of Palm Beach International Airport at the former West Palm Beach air base, and expansion at the port.

The complexion of business in the county changed in 1958, when the first major corporate entity staked a presence. Pratt & Whitney opened a 7,000-acre complex northwest of West Palm Beach to develop and test jet and rocket engines. That kick-started a trickle of big businesses and large-scale employers moving into the area. In 1961, RCA opened a $4 million plant in Palm Beach Gardens, a community developed by insurance tycoon John D. MacArthur. In 1967, a year after Interstate-95 reached the county, IBM opened a plant in Boca Raton. In 1981, a local team led by Philip "Don" Estridge developed the IBM PC, or personal computer, which revolutionized the industry. The Boca Raton plant then grew to massive proportions, employing almost 10,000. Other major new industries followed, including Motorola in Boynton Beach and Siemens in Boca Raton. This period also saw the coming of the area's first shopping malls and a new five-building terminal at the airport. County promotional brochures now promised fun and sun and, as one from 1969 reads, "clean blue-chip industry, big industrial parks, clean jobs." Between 1950 and 1970, the popula-

tion tripled, with a new-found phenomenon of people no longer just coming for a visit or the winter, but now living and working in the county year round.

Before long, Palm Beach County experienced a real estate boom unrivled in its history. It occurred in the mid-to late-1980s, largely fuel, among other factors, by the so-called "bull market" of the time and north-easterners — enjoying significant stock market gains — investing in second homes. Between 1987 and 1989, a flurry of planned luxury residential developments sprung up, particularly in Boca Raton and northern Palm Beach County, where undeveloped land was still in large supply. Between 1980 and 1990, the year-round population grew from 567,812 to 863,518. However, a national recession in 1991 briefly slowed growth. The construction industry came to a near standstill and bad weather hit agriculture in the western county.

Since the recession, the county's economy has continued to expand. Today, the number of business establishments grows by about 1,000 annually. Although many of them are small start-up companies, corporate operations continue to grow despite national downsizing trends. FPL and The Wackenhut Corporation moved their headquarters from Miami to the north county area, while W.R. Grace transferred its corporate headquarters from New York City to Boca Raton. Office Depot, third with over $3 billion in revenues in *Florida Trend's* top 250 public corporations, is a home grown product. Companies generally are lured by quality of life, favorable taxes, and programs providing grants for job creation and training, among other things. Some setbacks have occurred. IBM closed its Boca Raton campus and the area continues to look for a substitute for the blue-chip giant. Pratt & Whitney, among others, has downsized at alarming rates. In addition, while agriculture should continue its stable growth, the strong dollar could work against agricultural exports and lend support to imports.

A sampling of the current top forty companies in the county reveals that a number of key industries have emerged alongside agriculture, tourism, construction, and real estate: computers and communications, aerospace and engineering, medical products and pharmaceutical enterprises, and business services. The health services industry, bolstered by the strong presence of seniors and aging Baby Boomers, was the fastest-growing sector between 1985 and 1995, increasing by 102.9 percent. In the future, the financial sector is expected to join the leaders. For one thing, it too benefits from seniors — who account for about thirty percent of the population — and the high numbers of Baby Boomers, whose personal incomes continue to rise. Per capita personal income in the area is now about $38,000.

The financial sector will also benefit as foreign investment increases alongside international trade, which holds promise even though Palm Beach County is by no means an international banking metropolis like Miami. The Port of Palm Beach — the only South Florida port facility

Facing page: The post World War II era reinvigorated Palm Beach County's growth. From 1950 to 1970, the county's population tripled and a new trend toward year round residency emerged. From 1980 to 1990, the population grew from 567,812 to 863,518. The need to keep pace with that growth fueled the development of dynamic construction and real estate industries which continue to make a significant contribution to the region's economic mix. Photo The Weitz Company, Inc.

with its own rail system with pier-side rail box, hopper, and intermodal cars operating 24 hours a day — is now the fourth busiest port in Florida with $2 billion in goods passing through annually. Aggressive expansion plans at the port will facilitate much higher levels of trade. Meanwhile, some 31,000 tons of cargo pass through Palm Beach International Airport, one of the largest medium-hub airports in the United States with plans to expand its direct flights to destinations throughout the continental U.S., the Bahamas, and Canada and is to begin flights to Europe and South America.

While job growth in the 1990s has exceeded long-term projections — more than 16,000 in 1996 alone — and recent unemployment rates have been as low as any in the past decade, one area of concern in Palm Beach County as it enters the new century is indeed its work force. The head-spinning growth of high-tech firms requires an increasingly skilled and educated labor pool. The Palm Beach County Workforce Development Board, comprised of leaders in business, government, and community agencies, is addressing the issue with a number of initiatives, including training programs. Also being watched is the area's welfare-to-work program, a system of transitioning people from public assistance to full-time employment. For the first time in the county's history, that task has been put into the hands of the private sector as the state takes its first steps toward privatizing welfare and jobs programs. The outcome is uncertain.

Overall, though, the solid presence now of international and regional companies, as well as the future expansion of international trade, bodes well for Palm Beach County. Of United States metropolitan areas with a population over 500,000, the county ranked as the third-fastest growing MSA in the country, experiencing a growth rate of nearly fifty percent over the last decade. Certainly with such growth comes strained public dollars spread over numerous social and economic development initiatives. Grant money used for luring more business to the area — which comes from public coffers — has been the subject of debate and may dry up. But that is a relatively new initiative. Except for the early 1990s recession, business has grown with and without government grants for decades. Barring a severe national economic turndown — most business sectors in the county are expected to grow, and a budding global reach may tap more and more international business.

CHAPTER FOUR

Health Care In Palm Beach County

By M. M. Cloutier

Although most of Palm Beach county's pioneer settlers came to farm, some also came to find good health. While the year-round warm climate eased such ailments as rheumatism and asthma, the primitive, swampy conditions of the late 1800s inevitably bred other health problems. This prompted the community to seek a resident doctor — the first step in what has become one of the finest health care systems in Florida, serving the third fastest-growing metropolitan area in the nation. In fact, as far back as the 1920s when a heated hospital debate ensued, health care has

The littlest doctor attends her favorite patient. Palm Beach County has one of the most comprehensive and multifaceted health care systems in The United States. It boasts an abundance of quality facilities and services to care for its more than one million residents and hundreds of annual tourists. Photo Intracoastal Health Systems, Inc.

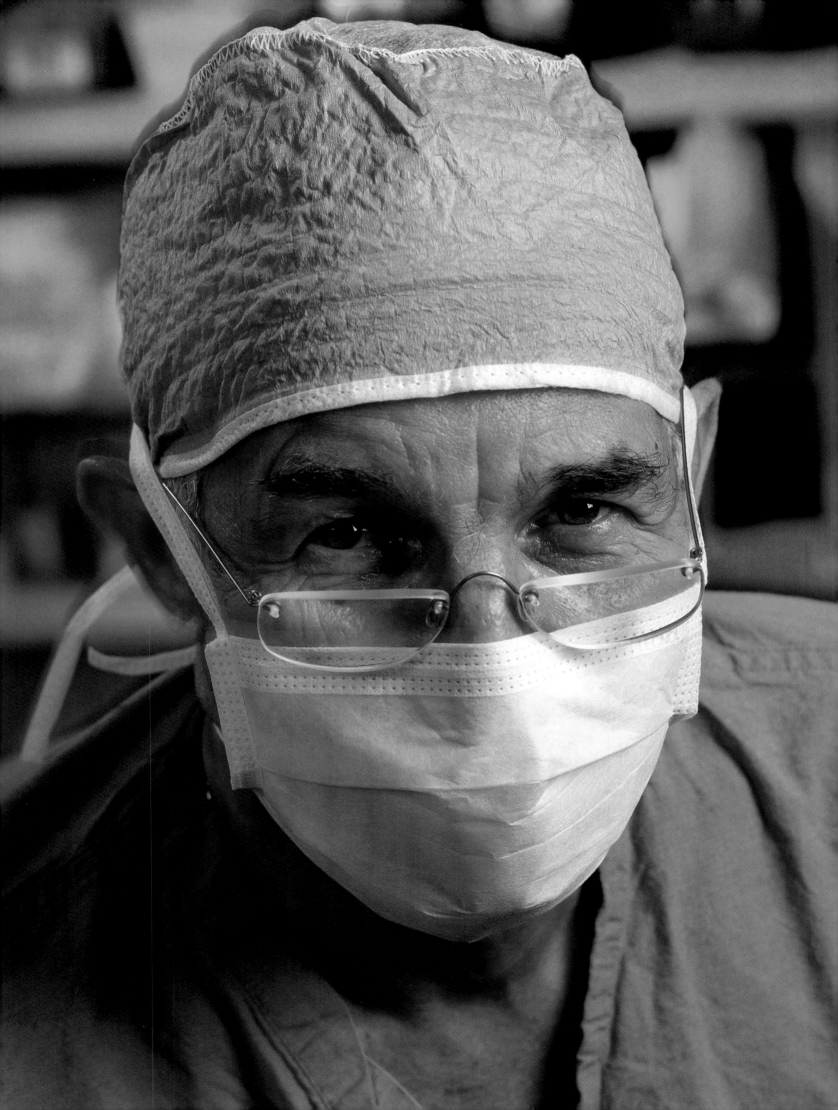

been among the county's chief priorities. This is especially true today as such factors as health care reform, the proliferation of health-maintenance organizations (HMOs), and the for-profit takeover of medicine, rapidly change the health care landscape.

In 1881, settlers in the "Lake country" — as Palm Beach County then was known — decided to find a doctor to serve their budding farming community, which had already faced many medical crises. Dr. Richard P. Potter, who had practiced medicine in Miami since 1874, decided to follow his brother to the Palm Beaches. Besides opening his practice, he also homesteaded many ocean front acres. Other doctors soon followed, as did quacks selling cure-alls in a jar. "Sanitariums," their solariums and baths, later opened in both Palm Beach and West Palm Beach. One sanitarium described itself as "equipped to take care of all cases, excepting those requiring operations." Typical cases included nervous conditions and substance abuse.

After the critical wounding of local deputy sheriff R.C. Baker in 1910, it became clear the area's more than 1,700 residents needed a hospital. County and city funds, as well as generous individual donations, built Emergency Hospital in 1914. This small one-story building with a porch, was located on what is now Fifth Street in West Palm Beach, near the city's Florida East Coast railway station. Emergency Hospital served only whites. African Americans patronized Pine Ridge Hospital, built a year later. Until the 1960s, health care remained segregated.

The area's population doubled between 1910 and 1915 and reached 19,000 by 1920, outgrowing the capacity and limited services of Emergency Hospital. As the real estate boom began, demographic pundits of the day predicted astronomical growth throughout the 1920s and many citizens clamored for a new, larger, and improved hospital. A $1,000 pledge by Colonel E.R. Bradley and his brother John, who owned the Beach Club, a posh gambling and dining spot in Palm Beach, spawned more contributions and helped gain state approval and backing. Good Samaritan Hospital, which today remains a key component in the county's health care, opened in 1920 with 35 beds at 12th Street in West Palm Beach, overlooking Lake Worth. Among the finest hospitals in the state, it received an "A" rating from the American College of Surgeons. Unfortunately, when the county's land boom, at its height between 1924 and 1925, busted, the hospital temporarily fell into troubled times along with the rest of the area's institutions, businesses, and residents.

About the same time Good Samaritan was unveiled, a convalescent home in Palm Beach for returning World War I veterans was also scheduled to open. The project, launched by Paris Singer

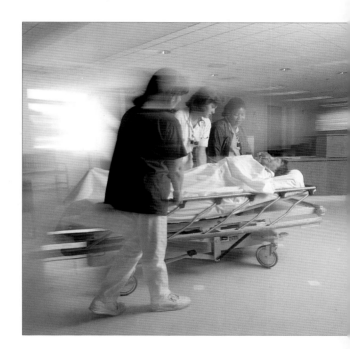

Nurses rush a patient to the Emergency Department. Immediate attention is a vital component in trauma units. Photo Intracoastal Health Systems, Inc.

Facing page: Neurosurgeon Eugene Holly, M.D. Palm Beach County has attracted many top notch professionals with valued skills and experience. Photo Intracoastal Health Systems, Inc.

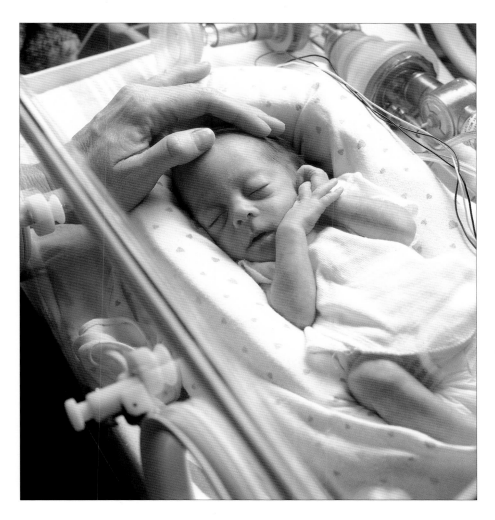

Excellent neonatal intensive care units are available for premature and critically ill infants. Photo Intracoastal Health Systems, Inc.

Facing page: Jubilant parents cradle their healthy new born infant. Photo Intracoastal Health System, Inc.

and Addison Mizner, who played influential roles in the early development of the area, never got off the ground, as few veterans wanted to leave their homes and families and travel to Palm Beach. After Singer gave its hospital equipment to Good Samaritan, the facility opened in 1919 as a private club instead: The Everglades, one of the most exclusive of its kind even today.

The key health care issue in the 1920s concerned the county's need for a second major hospital. The state legislature passed a bill calling for the hospital and a local committee, called the Palm Beach County General Hospital Association, to drum up support throughout the county. When it became known a state-of-the-art hospital could cost tax payers $750,000, a heated debate broke out. Proponents claimed the county's growth warranted a second hospital; opponents charged growth had stopped and Good Samaritan had far from reached capacity. In 1928, residents voted two-to-one against floating the $750,000 bond issue for the hospital.

The next new hospital came during World War II, when the U.S. Army, which had established two key air bases in the county, temporarily turned some of the area's hotels into hospitals. The most notable in Palm Beach was The Breakers Hotel which joined the war effort as Ream Army Hospital, treating wounded servicemen. Eleanor Roosevelt paid a visit in 1944.

Optimum health care is available for patients of all ages and sizes. Photo Intracoastal Health Systems, Inc.

Facing page: A few relaxing moments in the hospital playroom. Photo Intracoastal Health Systems, Inc.

Palm Beach County, experienced unprecedented growth between 1950 and 1970, when nearly 350,000 people called the area home. The health care industry also grew — particularly in the 1960s, which saw rampant health care expansion nationwide. Many analysts attribute this to the passage of Medicare and Medicaid in 1965. Palm Beach County had a half dozen hospitals in 1970. By 1985, there were twelve, serving communities from Jupiter to Boca Raton.

Today, Palm Beach County has a comprehensive, multi-faceted health care system that serves the needs of more than one million residents and hundreds of thousands of annual tourists. In fact, the health services industry became the fastest-growing business sector in the county between 1985 and 1995, with a 102.9 percent increase. Currently, among the thousands of health care professionals are more than 2,700 physicians and 800 dentists. There are also 48 nursing homes, 115 assisted living facilities, and 20 treatment centers. Those numbers continue to grow at a brisk pace alongside annual population growth.

The county now boasts fifteen hospitals, which far exceed present needs. Combined, the hospitals provide comprehensive services — from the common to the highly specialized, including everything from nuclear medicine, coronary care, cancer care, bone marrowing/stem cell transplant, and acute dialysis to obstetrics, perinatolog, neonatal care, neurology, and hyperbaric medicine.

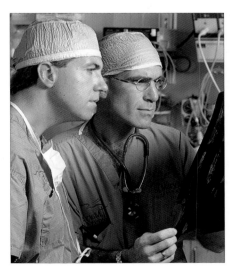

Surgeons Richard Rodman, M.D., and Jack Daubert, M.D., offer specialized treatment for those in need. Photo Intracoastal Health Systems, Inc.

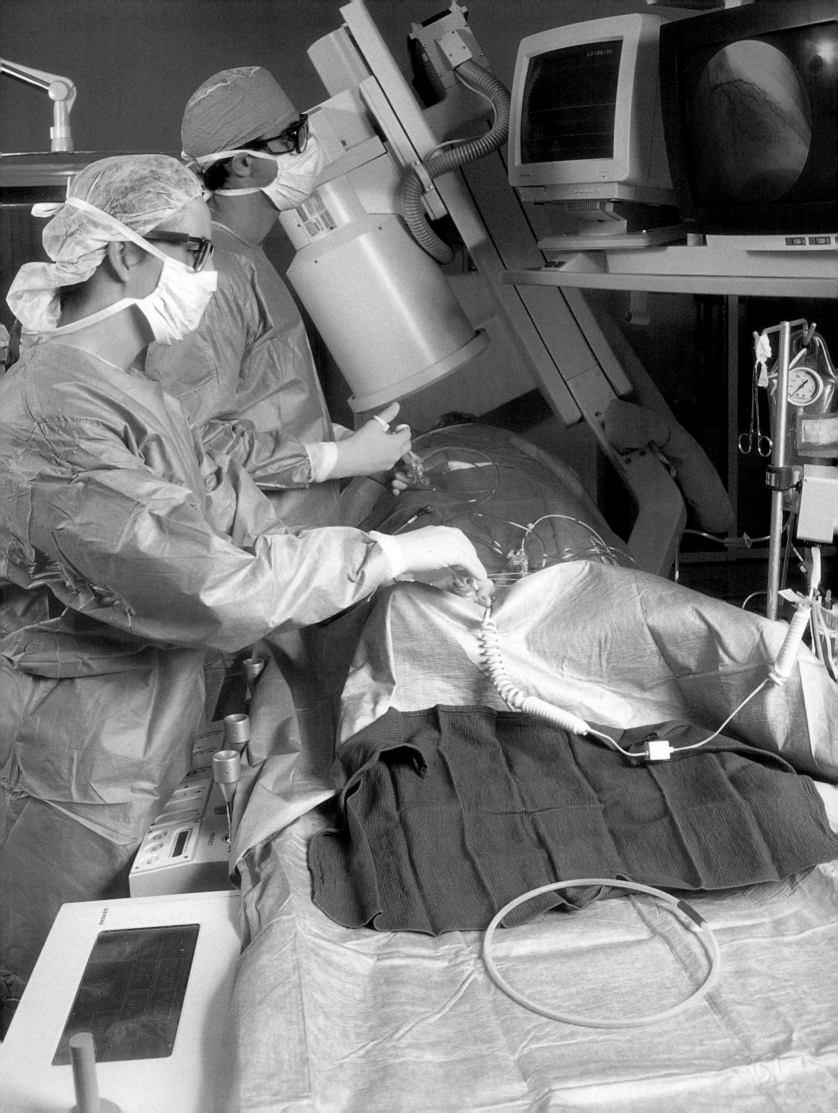

The hospitals weathered a rocky, road in the late 1980s and early 90s, a period marked by government enforcement of tough new restrictions on Medicare payments and increased competition. Another key factor in recent years has been hospital mergers and acquisitions. In 1990, most of the county's hospitals remained independent and non-profit. Now half are connected to for-profit hospital chains based elsewhere in the country. A trend in many areas of the country, Palm Beach County is particularly attractive to chains with its growing population and large concentration of both wealthy people and Medicare recipients.

Seven of the area's fifteen hospitals now are for-profit facilities. Nashville-based Columbia/HCA Healthcare Corporation owns Columbia Hospital in West Palm Beach (250 beds), Palms West Hospital in Loxahatchee (117 beds) and JFK Medical Center in Atlantis, a 363 bed facility, recognized as one of the top one hundred hospitals in the USA. With several Ambulatory Centers, over 440 staff, more than 2,500 employees and an active volunteer auxiliary, JFK offers a full compliment of services with the exception of obstetrics and pediatrics. Santa Monica, California-based Tenet Healthcare Corp., also owns three hospitals: Delray Medical Center (224 beds), Palm Beach Gardens Medical Center (204 beds) and West Boca Medical Center (185 beds). Wellington Regional Medical Center (120 beds) is owned by Universal Health Services of King of Prussia, Pennsylvania.

Five hospitals remain non-profit, including Boca Raton Community Hospital, (394 beds). Boca Raton Community is the largest hospital in southern Palm Beach County and offers many specialized services, some of which include: the nationally recognized Lynn Regional Cancer Center; the Women's Center and Center for Breast Care; One Family Place maternity and pediatrics; Surgicenter Plus and Pain Management Service; a Rapid Care Center; The Therapy Center; Outpatient Nutrition Center and Home Health Service. Located in Boynton Beach, Bethesda Memorial Hospital is a 362 bed facility that provides a complete spectrum of medical services with over 400 physicians and surgeons that practice in more than 30 specialty areas. Bethesda's complete continuum of care includes a: state-of-the-art Emergency Department; Ambulatory Care Unit; (same day surgery) Cardiac Care Services Center for Advanced Imaging; Behavioral Medicine Center; Vascular Institute; Fitness Center; Rehabilitation Facility; Transitional Care Unit; Home Care Network; Women's Health Services; Maternity Center; FirstBorn Program; Pediatric Unit; Neonatal Intensive Care

Facing page: Up to date medical facilities and state-of-the-art procedures are readily available in Palm Beach County. Photo JFK Medical Center.

Barbara Cooper, coordinator of The Cancer Institute at Good Samaritan Medical Center's "Friend to Friend" Cancer Patient Support Program, with Kirk Schiner, the first patient at The Cancer Institute's Bone Marrow/Stem Cell Transplant Program. Photo Intracoastal Health Systems, Inc.

Cancer survivor and Cancer Patient Support Program volunteer Marion Hicks. Photo Intracoastal Health Systems, Inc.

Facing page: New facilities, state-of-the-art technology and specialized medical professionals indicate that quality health care will remain a constant in Palm Beach County's future. Photo JFK Medical Center.

A nurse educator trains healthcare professionals as well as the general public in everything from CPR techniques to new medical technology. Photo Intracoastal Health Systems, Inc.

Unit and Genetic Counseling Services. Jupiter Medical Center has 156 beds, St. Mary's Medical Center in West Palm Beach has 433 beds and Good Samaritan, has grown from its inception in 1920 from 35 to 342 beds. Good "Sam" merged with St. Mary's in 1994, forming Intracoastal Health Systems, the largest not-for-profit hospital system in the county.

Two quasi-public hospitals operate in the Glades in western Palm County: Everglades Regional Center in Pahokee (63 beds) and Glades General Hospital in Belle Glade (73 beds). For years public health officials have tried to merge the two facilities, which may eventually happen. Palm Beach County's newest hospital, the federal Veterans Affairs Medical Center (400 beds plus a 120-bed nursing home), opened a state-of-the-art facility in 1995 in Riviera Beach serving 267,000 veterans throughout the South Florida region.

Aside from the new VA center, nearly all of the hospitals in the county have undergone major expansions and renovations during the past decade as health care becomes increasingly more competitive. That has been a strain on some, particularly the not-for-profits, though ultimately a major benefit to patients, who can count on services that employ quality doctors and equipment and keeps pace with medical technology. The spate of expansions crested in 1995, with Good "Sam's" new 22,000-square-foot emergency room and surgical center. Five Palm Beach donors contributed an astonishing $10 million which paid half the construction cost.

Trauma care has been a part of the county's health care system since 1988, when a special taxing body created the Palm Beach County Health Care District. The district supports two trauma centers at St. Mary's Hospital and Delray Community Hospital, each staffed 24 hours a day by trauma doctors. When necessary, the district's fully equipped helicopter ambulance, Trauma Hawk, is available. The district also provides medical services for people without health insurance, or covered by other programs, everything from emergency room visits to inpatient and outpatient care.

Key health care issues facing the county include health care reform in general, and the problems brought on by reduced Medicare spending, mostly through reductions in payments to hospitals and managed care groups. The proliferation of HMOs, which have been swooping down on the area for more than a decade, continues to raise many questions, especially about the kind of care members receive. The for-profit movement in medicine is another concern. Some industry analysts expect that by the year 2000, the majority of hospitals in Palm Beach County will be owned by for-profit chains, which seek to serve both patients and their shareholders.

Changes in today's health care industry are inevitable. But if the past is prologue in Palm Beach County, where since the 1920s health care has been among the finest in the state, quality health care will remain constant.

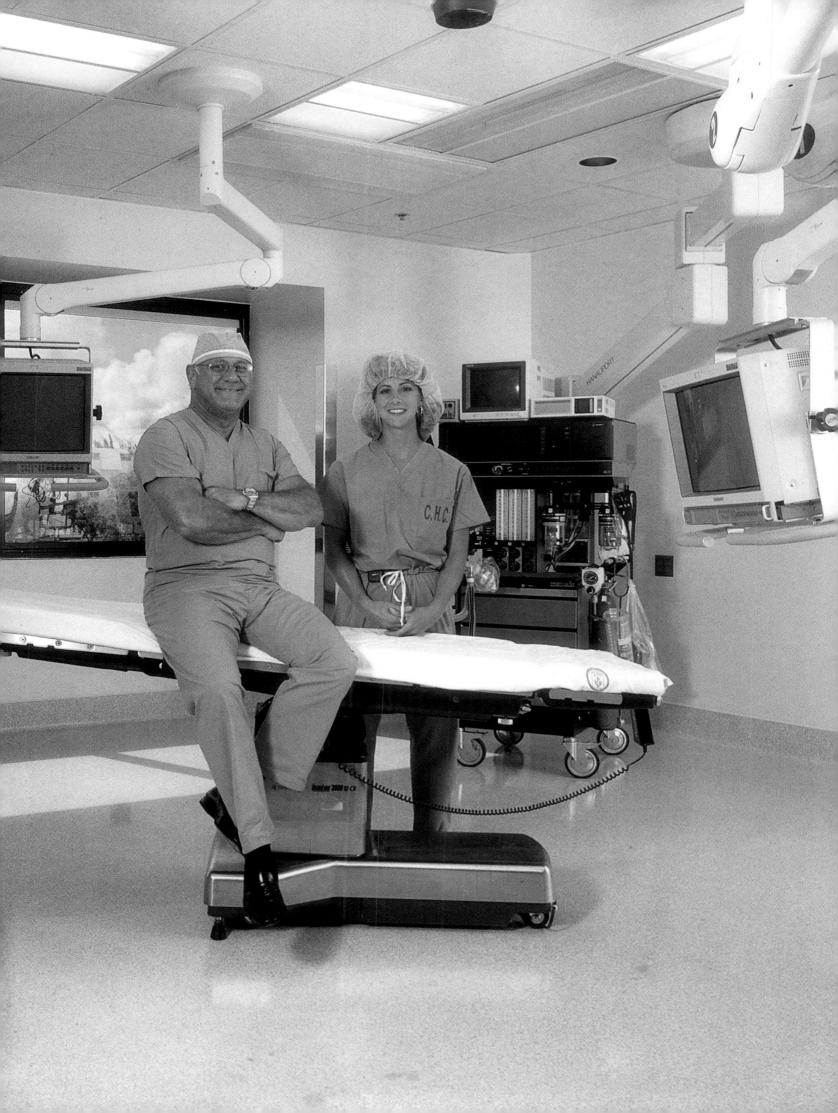

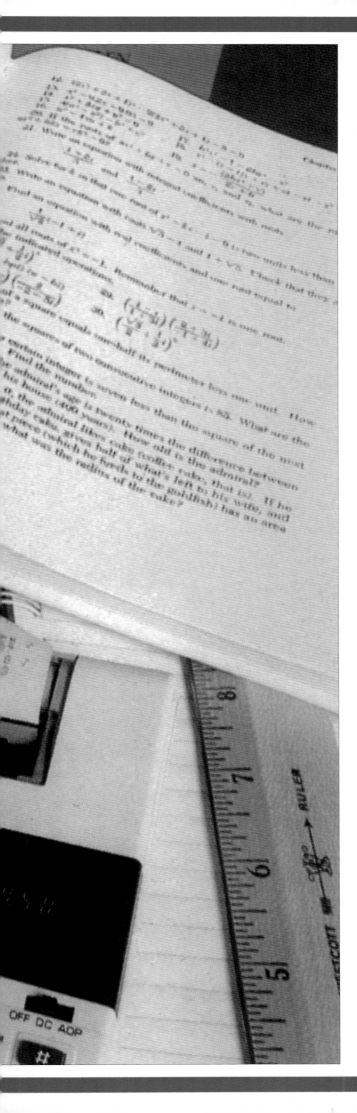

The Power Of Education

By Donald W. Curl, Ph.D.

The 1880s saw the arrival of many pioneer settlers to the country around Lake Worth. Since most came with their families, the numbers of children increased to the point where the settlers demanded a school. Since the area was still part of Dade County, they appealed to their county commissioners in Miami, who in 1886 agreed to pay the teacher's salary if the settlers would build and furnish the schoolhouse. Sixteen-year-old Hattie Gale, who taught her first class in March 1886, had students ranging in age from six to seventeen.

Today that little one-room school house, completely restored with the aid of the Preservation

The public school system with a budget of over a billion dollars is one of the largest in the country serving almost one-quarter-million students. Educational opportunities have grown right along with the county. Today, students can enter kindergarten and, without leaving Palm Beach County, continue their studies all the way to doctorate level. Photo Lynn University.

Foundation of Palm Beach, can be found in Phipps Ocean Park. Several times a week fourth graders from county schools come to experience a pioneer school day of the 19th century. Teachers from the foundation, dressed in appropriate costumes, conduct lessons on morality, honesty, and good manners. "The scholars leave here more polite and well-mannered calling their teacher 'Ma'am' and answering in full sentences," said a foundation instructor.

A four-room frame schoolhouse at Dixie Highway and Clematis Street served the new town of West Palm Beach in its early days, though the community had outgrown this school and classrooms used at the Congregational Church when the modern $50,000 schoolhouse on the hilltop site west of downtown opened in 1909. Built on land donated by pioneer settler Ellen Potter, parents originally feared its far western location might make their small children prey to alligators and other wild animals. In the year the school opened, Palm Beach County had been carved from the northern part of Dade and the new "central school" was the only one in the county. Although the original schoolhouse contained all twelve grades, as the population of young people grew, the school board erected a second building to house a junior high school. Finally, in 1923 Palm Beach High was built to the north of the original central school.

The land boom and the frenzy of growth in county population in the early and mid-1920s brought construction of new schools from Jupiter to Boca Raton to Pahokee. By the end of the land boom, the district had a system of over twenty schools. The bust and the coming of the national depression hit county schools very hard. In 1929 the school board could guarantee teachers only eight of their nine months' salaries. With accreditation threatened, the PTA stepped in and raised the money for high school teachers. Nonetheless, the problems continued and as late as November 1933 the school board negotiated a bank loan of $45,000 to pay teachers and school bus drivers.

As the financial struggle continued through the 1930s, the board constructed only a minimum of new schools. Then during World War II, the Army Air Corps stationed thousands of air men at the radar training school at the Boca Raton base and at Morrison Field in West Palm Beach. After the war many of these returned, setting off a new land boom that continues even today. The school board added thirty schools during the late 1940s and 1950s. In fact, the *Palm Beach Post* pointed out that by 1960 the county system employed more teachers than the total number of students in 1909 and operated 77 schools with a total budget of over $20 million. The board built thirty more schools in the 1960s. Still, construction rarely met demand, and portable classrooms surrounding local schools seemed like a way of life in the county.

In the years after the war, the housing problems of the school board were compounded by the system of segregation, which at least theoretically, called for equal but separate facilities for the races. Actually, one of the

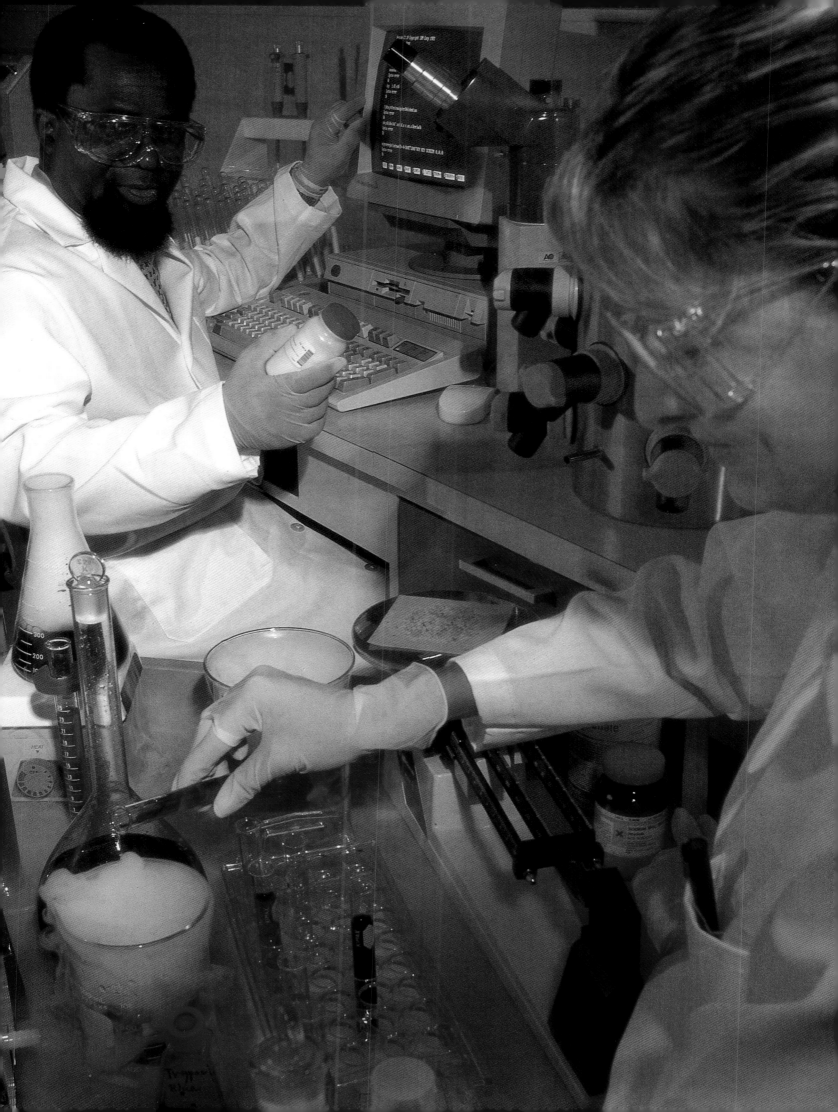

first battles in the civil rights wars was fought in Palm Beach County. In 1941 the Palm Beach County school board gave white teachers a raise without extending it to the county's African-American teachers. At the time, white teachers received $140 a month and black teachers $100. A black teachers' group organized by educator C. Spencer Pompey, decided to challenge the school board. Thurgood Marshall, starting his civil rights career as an attorney for the National Association for the Advancement of Colored People, represented the teachers. U.B. Kinsey, later principal of Palmview Elementary School, recalled that Marshall "made jackasses out of the school board's attorneys." The judge ruled for the teachers citing separate but equal doctrines and ordered the school board to pay black teachers the same salary as white teachers. This case helped set precedents for Marshall to use in winning *Brown v Board of Education* in 1954.

A year after *Brown*, the court told local districts to admit children "on a racially non-discriminatory basis with all deliberate speed." Vivian Rouson-Gossett and C. Spencer Pompey in *Like a Mighty Banyan, Contributions of Black People to the History of Palm Beach County* say this ruling had no effect on local schools. In fact, the board founded two new black high schools and Roosevelt Junior College after the ruling.

Local African-American leaders realized that the school board planned to ignore the *Brown* decision and decided to file suit in 1956. *Holland and Holland v Board of Public Instruction* dragged through the court system for a decade before the school board was ordered to integrate both faculty and students. Although a few African-American students attended white schools as early as 1961 under a "Freedom of Choice" option, only the court order brought plans to truly integrate the system. Unfortunately, these plans often proved a mixed blessing. "Integration" often meant phasing out black schools and the demotion of black faculty and administrators.

During the years of the great depression, Palm Beach County did gain its first institution of higher learning. In the early depression years, Howell Lee Watkins, the principal of Palm Beach High School, discovered that many graduates, unable to secure jobs, tried to return to high school for additional training. Howell persuaded Joseph Youngblood, superintendent of schools, to help him provide training for students seeking schooling beyond the high school level. The two men spoke to business and civic groups which then named representatives to an advisory board. The board and school officials in 1933 established Palm Beach Junior College, the state's first.

High school teachers with master's degrees volunteered to teach during their free time periods, after school, and on Saturdays. Watkins allowed the use of classrooms on the second floor of one of the high school buildings on Gardenia Street. Seventeen students enrolled for the first semester in the autumn of 1933 and thirty more joined them before the end of the month. During this year the teachers received no pay, though occasionally the board offered a five-dollar supplement to their regular salary.

The rich diversity of the county's people and professional opportunities has earned its rightful place in the education system. Photos Florida Atlantic University.

Youngblood served as president and Watkins as dean, a post he held for fifteen years.

Although the college offered no formal degree program in its first years, the University of Florida and Florida State College for Women (today's Florida State University) helped develop a curriculum that allowed transfers to the senior institutions. Many other Florida schools also accepted the work completed at the junior college.

In 1937, due largely to the efforts of John I. Leonard who succeeded Youngblood as superintendent and college president, the state legislature gave the county authority to support a junior college. With a guarantee of public funds, the school began the process towards accreditation which the Southern Association of Colleges and Schools granted in 1942.

The college remained on Gardenia Street until after World War II. Returning veterans and the GI-Bill brought rapid growth. To house this enlarged enrollment, the college purchased 21 acres on the deactivated Morrison Field from the United States government. The old base hospital became classrooms and administrative offices, the officers' club the student union, and officers' quarters new student dormitories.

A college history says the new campus provided an air of permanency, though one ruthfully shattered by the outbreak of the Korean conflict. War meant the Air Force reactivated Morrison Field and evicted the college. Its search for a new home took it to the town hall of Lake Park in August 1951. Originally built during the Florida real estate boom days as the municipal building for Kelsey City, its space was severely limited, forcing the college to reduce enrollment to 325 students.

Finally, after four years in the cramped quarters, the legislature appropriated development funds for the four existing state junior colleges. Of the funds, Palm Beach Junior College received over one-million dollars. The county commission offered the institution a 114-acre site in Lake Worth and construction began on a group of modern buildings to house administration, library, classrooms, laboratories, engineering, fine arts, physical education, student union, and a cafeteria. President Leonard moved his college to the Lake Worth campus in September 1956, beginning a continuing era of expansion and growth for the school.

During Palm Beach Junior College's 25th-anniversary year in 1958 Harold C. Manor became president and enrollment topped 1,000. As Palm Beach County and its institutions still remained strictly segregated, this year also saw the founding of Roosevelt Junior College for African Americans. Beginning with afternoon and evening classes at the all-black Roosevelt High School, the junior college gave young African Americans the opportunity to attend college in the county. Although the college secured its own buildings on 15th Street in West Palm Beach, it never had an enrollment larger than 300. When the courts ordered Palm Beach County schools to integrate, the school board made the black school a branch of Palm Beach Junior College, and in 1965 closed it entirely. Of the

Palm Beach County students are served by one of the largest public school systems in the country as well as a wealth of private institutions. Photo C. J. Walker.

The Dolly Hand Cultural Arts Center. Photo Palm Beach Community College.

eighteen African-American faculty members, only six were transferred to Palm Beach Junior College. One of these, Daniel Hendrix, became the first African American elected to the school board.

In 1968 the state legislature separated Florida's junior colleges from their local school boards. For Palm Beach, this meant that the college's advisory board now became its board of trustees, overseeing its management and budget. In that year the student body also grew to over 5,000 and the Lake Worth campus seemed as cramped as had the Lake Park town hall.

In 1978 Edward M. Eissey became president with the mission to expand the college into new areas of the county. Although the college owned a building in Belle Glade, a campus was now developed with the Dolly Hand Cultural Arts Center at its heart. Since then the college has established a full campus on PGA Boulevard in Palm Beach Gardens and one on the Florida Atlantic University campus in Boca Raton.

In 1988 the school's board of trustees changed its name to Palm Beach Community College. President Eissey called for the change as he said, "the word junior connotes incompleteness and [our] range of services to the community goes far beyond that." Today Palm Beach Community College serves over 40,000 students on four major campuses in the county.

Just as Palm Beach County became home to the state's first junior college, so too it received the first university in south Florida when the 1955 legislature authorized the Board of Control, then governing body of the state's system of higher education, to plan for a new university on the southeastern coast. To many, the old Boca Raton air field, largely abandoned since the 1947 hurricane, presented the ideal site for a new university. Located near the Broward County line, it could conveniently draw students from the entire southeastern coastal area. Moreover, the base's 1,250 acres ensured space for future expansion.

The Board of Control selected the Boca Raton site when consultants claimed that over 30,000 potential students lived only an hour's drive away. Thomas F. Fleming, Jr., lead the local campaign to bring the university to Boca Raton. Once the Board of Control approved, Fleming now had to convince the federal government to give the state the land.

Fleming, a real estate developer and founder of the First Bank and Trust Company (now Nationsbank), had moved to Boca Raton in 1939 after his marriage to Myrtle Butts, to help manage her family's farms. He became active in civic affairs and served on the town council. His father, a lawyer and banker, had moved the family to Fort Lauderdale from

Palm Beach Junior College, now known as Palm Beach Community College, opened in 1933 as the county's first institute of higher learning and the state's first junior college. Photo Palm Beach Community College.

Georgia during the land boom. In 1938 the younger Fleming graduated from the University of Florida where his fellow students elected him president of the senior class and selected him for membership in Blue Key, the leadership honorary. At the time, George Smathers, the future senator, and Paul Rogers, the future congressman, were also members. Fleming used his friendships with Smathers and Rogers to gain the contacts with the Civil Aeronautics Administration which gave the state 1,000 acres with the proviso that the university be established by 1969. It set aside the remaining land for a civilian airport.

Although original plans for the university called for a traditional four-year institution, the planning committee report issued in 1961 now called for an upper division school of juniors, seniors, and graduate students to mesh with and complete the work of Florida's growing members of junior colleges. With extensive use of new technology, faculty members were to gain time for closer contacts with students and for their own research. The technology included an automated library, student "work stations" taking advantage of both audio and televised information sources, and televised lectures.

When it came time for the state legislature to provide funds for construction, Panhandle "porkchoppers" in control of the legislative process acting on the traditional premise that south Florida should pay the taxes to be spent by and for north Florida, demanded a new university in Pensacola before one in Boca Raton. Since the legislature had ordered the university to open in 1964, the Board of Control called upon the local community to raise $100,000 for planning and architectural fees to meet this deadline. Fleming headed the committee that raised this money and also paid the salaries of the president and other officials before the university opened.

When state officials came to realize the deplorable conditions found on all university campuses, the legislature finally authorized a $25-million bond issue for additions to the four existing universities and to build the new Boca Raton campus. The bonds sold in 1962 and the new school received $5.3 million for construction.

The Board of Control now decided to name the new institution, which had received the popular name "Boca U." The board called for a name symbolic of the entire southeast. Unfortunately, it had already named an institution in the central part of the state the University of South Florida. A newspaper poll brought forth such suggestions as Palm State, Peninsula, Gulfstream, Kennedy of Florida, and in recognition of the space program, A-Okay university. At its May 1962 meeting the Board of Control chose Florida Atlantic University and also named Kenneth Rash Williams, the founding head of Miami-Dade Community College, its first president. Willliams, a Florida native, arrived in Boca Raton in July 1962 and set up offices in the air base's old fire station.

On Sunday afternoon, June 21, 1964, 10,000 visitors toured the completed library, science laboratory, television, classroom, and utility buildings on the new campus. As the new faculty began moving into their offices, they realized that the state had no intention of providing adequate funding for the school's innovative program. As Roger H. Miller, the first dean of administrative affairs, said in his memoirs: "The seed of experimentation, rather than being nurtured was, from the very outset, treated like a bonsai tree, pruned to the edge of extinction."

Nonetheless, the faculty continued to plan a curriculum utilizing television courses and other experimental techniques and the university adopted the motto "Where Tomorrow Begins." Unfortunately, hurricane Cleo postponed that beginning. With classes scheduled for September 8, Cleo hit the southeast Florida coast, rescheduling the opening to September 14. Moreover, early studies had predicted the enrollment of 2,500 students. Only 800 students actually enrolled. Hindsight attributed this to a serious lack of recruiting, the failure of the university to provide dormitory and eating facilities on campus and the lack of rooms and apartments in Boca Raton, combined with no public transportation system and the exceeding poor south Florida roads.

President Lyndon B. Johnson came to Boca Raton on October 25 to preside over the dedication ceremony for the university. In a speech before 15,000 people, Johnson, campaigning for reelection, called for "a new revolution in education" to open college doors to all who qualified. Johnson also received the University's first honorary degree.

Williams served as president until 1973 when Glenwood Creech, the vice president for university relations at the University of Kentucky, became FAU's second president. Under Creech's leadership the university funded four Eminent Scholar chairs through a program in which the state added $400,000 to every $600,000 raised by the university. It also received several endowed professorships and major gifts for specific projects, such as Thomas Fleming's bequest of 63 paintings of Florida artist A.E. "Beanie" Backus and the gift of Lullis and Rolland Ritter to build an art gallery.

When president Creech retired in 1983, his replacement, Helen Popovich, became the first woman to hold a university presidency in the state system. In 1984, FAU added freshmen and sophomore classes, ending the upper-division experiment. Popovich also championed the university's affirmative action program and under her encouragement more women and members of minority groups joined FAU's faculty and administration.

In 1987 Popovich resigned and accepted the presidency of a small state university in Michigan. Anthony J. Catanese, dean of the University of Florida's College of Architecture, became FAU's fourth president in 1988. He is known for championing inter-collegiate sports and his aggressive concern for fund raising. Under his leadership the sports program entered the National Collegiate Athletic Association's Division I, and the university received its largest donation. Charles Schmidt, who with his wife Dorothy had already endowed chairs in engineering and the performing arts, announced a gift of $10 million at a 1992 convocation. The gift, to honor

Private institutions such as Lynn and Norwood Universities and Palm Beach Atlantic College have expanded the horizons of higher learning first charted in the county by Palm Beach Community College and Florida Atlantic University. Photos Lynn University.

Dorothy who had died in 1991, called for the building of the Dorothy E. Schmidt Center for the Arts and the establishment of two "super chairs." Since the state matched the gift, the university actually received $20 million.

In September 1963, a year before FAU opened, Marymount College held its first classes in Palm Beach County. One of five colleges of the Religious of the Sacred Heart of Mary, it provided a "two-year college. . . for young women." An all-purpose academic building named for Miami's Bishop Coleman F. Carrol, a student center called Founders Hall, a dormitory, and utilities building welcomed the first students. The 65-acre campus on Military Trail in Boca Raton contained room for future expansion.

Mother M. Joques became the institution's first president, although Mother de la Croix, who directed the campus building program, soon succeeded as head of the college. She saw the student body grow to around 500 during her administration. The college also added two additional dormitories and a new library-learning resources building.

Unfortunately, the school never attracted enough students to become financially successful. In 1971 Wilmington College of New Castle, Delaware, took over the struggling institution, changing its name to the

College of Boca Raton. Donald Ross became president of the now non-sectarian school. In 1974 the college added the junior and senior years and began awarding baccalaureate degrees. It has also offered innovative programs in geriatrics and hospitality manage ment. In 1995, in recognition of the many gifts of Eugene and Christine Lynn, the college changed its name to Lynn University.

The 1960s became a decade for higher education in Palm Beach County. Joining Florida Atlantic and Marymount, Palm Beach Atlantic College opened its doors in1968. Founded by the Reverend Jess Moody, pastor of West Palm Beach's First Baptist Church, the Baptist school pioneered a program called "workship" that required its students to perform public service as well as attend classes. Starting with 85 students in classrooms in the original church building on South Olive Avenue, the school has grown to almost 2,000students today.

Moody served as president for Palm Beach Atlantic's first six years and left the area in 1976 to become pastor of a large church in suburban Los Angeles. His successors brought the school into a more traditional academic pattern, though 45 of public service work beyond the classroom is still required. Paul Corts, its current president, has been an active fund raiser in the area.

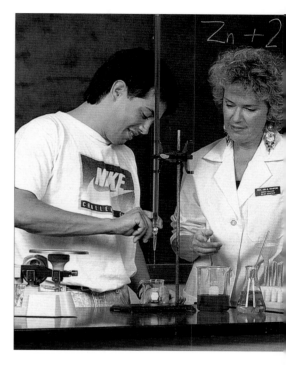

Although the college considered moving to the west of the city where it could purchase less expensive land, by 1980s it had decided to stay in the section south of downtown. In 19882 the trustees spent $2.5 million for a new Lassiter Student Center, added Sachs Hall (administration), Vivian Johnson Residence Hall, and the Catherine T. MacArthur classroom building at a $8.2 million cost in 1989. The $5.2 million Rinker Hall housing the business school and a dormitory opened in 1991, and another student dormitory, Baxter Hall, was completed in 1995. These projects were possible because of many generous gifts, including $14.4 million from Theodore R. Johnson, a retired United Parcel Service executive. The college plans to continue its expansion on its 25-acre campus along South Dixie Highway, adding a new physical education complex and a music and fine arts building just north of Norton Museum.

Today the education choices in Palm Beach County seem unending. The public school system with a budget of over a billion dollars is one of the largest in the country serving almost one-quarter-million students. A Roman Catholic school system furnishes parochial education through high school, and other religious groups support schools throughout the county. First -rate preparatory schools from Boca Raton's Saint Andrews to North Palm Beach's Benjamin School provide the best of private education. Higher education is supplied by the private Lynn and Northwood universities and Palm Beach Community College and Florida Atlantic University. A Palm Beach County student can enter a kindergarten program and without leaving the county, continue all the way to the doctorate degree.

CHAPTER SIX

Breaking The News

By Millie Wolff

Take the funnies, but don't mess up the rest of the newspaper, is seldom heard throughout the land these days. Today the kids are probably watching cartoons on TV, though more than likely Dad still reads the paper with his morning coffee.

The Palm Beach Post is the arbiter of the news in Palm Beach County. Seven days each week a-half-million readers from north to south, from east to west find out what's new locally, county wide, and in Tallahassee and Washington from *The Post*. They discover the ups and downs of the market, foreign affairs, opinions of William Safire, George Will, William Raspberry, and other pundits who help their fellow-

"Each morning, more than 500,000 residents in Palm Beach County and the Treasure Coast wake up to the award winning Palm Beach Post." Since 1889, *Palm Beach County's local media have contributed to the civic and cultural life of the community while fulfilling their mission to keep residents up-to-date on vital news, society happenings and important issues. Photo The Palm Beach Post.*

men decide what they are for and what they are against. According to Walter Cronkite, "the words from an average thirty minute newscast would fill roughly only two-thirds of a newspaper page."

The first newspaper in what became Palm Beach County was the Tropical Sun, though some readers insisted upon calling it the "Prodigal Son." Guy I. Metcalf, who published the Indian River News in Melbourne, agreed to move his newspaper to Juno in 1889. The year before Dade County voters had approved the removal of the county seat from Miami to almost non-existent Juno. One of the first buildings erected in the new town, a two-story, twenty-by-forty-foot structure, became the home of the newspaper.

Henry Flagler and his railway by-passed Juno, the southern stop on the legendary seven-and-a-half-mile long Celestial Railroad. When Flagler developed West Palm Beach, Metcalf saw a troubled future for Juno, and moved his paper to the new city. Five years later, the voters proved Metcalf correct when the county seat once more returned to Miami.

Metcalf, an outspoken editor and publisher, called for the building of a road to Miami and after the county seat's return to that town, campaigned for the formation of a new county in northern Dade. This campaign bore fruit in 1909 when the Florida legislature created Palm Beach County. Although never a major daily, the Tropical Sun continued publication until the end of the 1920s land boom.

D.H. Conkling founded the Palm Beach Post in 1908 as a weekly. In 1916 it became a daily, and like all south Florida newspapers, its paid advertisements soared during the years of the Land Boom. Frank P. Fildes began publishing an evening newspaper, the Palm Beach Times, in 1922 to take advantage of the land boom. When the boom busted, both newspapers suffered lean years. With the coming of the national depression their owners decided to join forces. At the time Sheriff Robert Baker owned the Times. They also borrowed $100,000 from colorful Colonel E.R. Bradley, the proprietor of the Beach Club, Palm Beach's gambling casino.

When the financial situation of the newspapers failed to improve, Bradley assumed ownership in 1934. He assigned his long-time business associate, C. Barry Shannon, as publisher. Although Bradley willed the two newspapers to Shannon, only a few months after Bradley's death in 1945, Shannon also died.

In 1947 long-time Palm Beach resident John Holliday Perry, Sr., purchased the newspapers from Shannon's estate for just over one-million dollars. Perry owned a Florida newspaper chain which included six dailies and fifteen weeklies. In homage to his adopted state, in 1925 he and Frank Parker Stockbridge had co-authored Florida in the Making to "tell the true story of Florida." It became a national best seller.

In 1948 Perry also acquired the Palm Beach Daily News (originally the Lake Worth News) and Palm Beach Life magazine from Oscar G. Davies. Davies's father, Richard Overend Davies had founded the magazine and

Palm Beach Daily News, Saturday, April 27, 1996

Style

Interiors, Gardening & Lifestyles

n Marjorie Merriweather Post's day, guests dined at an immense marble-topped table, which was sold to make way for more intimate club dining. However, the room's spectacular murals, from frescoes at the Chigi Palace in Rome, are unchanged. They depict a variety of allegorical nautical scenes. The Capo di Monte china and blue Venetian glassware belonged to Post used only for Mar-a-Lago Club special events. **Above, top left:** Join Mar-a-Lago Club for $75,000 and you still have to pay $1,000 a night to stay in the best rooms in the house, such as the Room. But where else would you get to sleep with medieval ladies-in-waiting posing in the arches of the beehive fireplace? Heraldic symbols glow from the painted coffered ceiling. Most

purchased the newspaper in 1905 with the financial backing of Henry Flagler. Both father and son supported civic improvement projects and spearheaded the movement for the construction of the town's Memorial Fountain.

Ruby Edna Pierce joined the newspaper in 1907. In 1910 she became editor and general manager of both Palm Beach Daily News and Palm Beach Life, posts she continued to hold until she retired in 1954. During these 44 years she made "The Shiny Sheet" (the News is printed on shiny high grade stock to keep the ink from rubbing-off on the readers' hands while they eat breakfast) the respectable society news source in the resort.

The Palm Beach Daily News, affectionately referred to as "The Shiny Sheet", proves its reputation as the source for society news with coverage of Donald Trump's newly redecorated Mar-a-Largo. Photo C. J. Walker.

Palm Beach Life

February 1, 1927

Price 25 cents

The Weekly Journal of Society

Although John H. Perry, Jr. continued to run the Florida newspaper chain after his father's death in 1952, eventually he became more interested in marine research and in building small submarines for this research. In 1969 he sold all of his West Palm Beach and Palm Beach publications to Cox Enterprises for an estimated $20 million. Cox Enterprises, founded by former Ohio governor and 1920 Democratic party presidential candidate James M. Cox, is today a vast media empire based in Atlanta, Georgia, that includes twenty daily newspapers as well as radio and television stations. James Cox had owned the Miami News since the early 1920s. A cost saving measure of Cox Enterprises combined the two West Palm Beach newspapers on weekends as the Palm Beach Post-Times. In the late 1980s the Times, which remained a daily evening newspaper, joined the trend of afternoon editions and was merged with the morning Post. The Cox chain also continues to publish the Palm Beach Daily News.

The Palm Beach Post takes its community responsibility seriously and sponsors more than 150 community events throughout Palm Beach, Martin, and St. Lucie counties. These events range from educational (science fairs and teacher recognition programs) to cultural (ArtiGras, Sunfest, and Bookfest) to sporting events (PGA Seniors Golf Tournament and Virginia Slims Legends Tournament).

In addition the Community Relations department coordinates the Post's own community programs such as Pathfinder Scholarship Program, Spelling Bee, Law Officers of the Year Awards, building tours, and a speaker's bureau.

Since 1897 the Palm Beach Daily News has brought community affairs, scandal, society, formal balls, and gossip to the residents of the resort town with a population of about 10,000 that triples during the season. The paper rarely changes, although recently it added an editorial page.

On the occasion of its centennial celebration on February 7, 1997, it included a letter from President Bill Clinton among the many congratulatory messages. Rumor has it that along with the New York Times, Wall Street Journal, and other national newspapers, the White House has a subscription to the Palm Beach Daily News. It has never claimed to be other than a community newspaper. But what a community! National and international personalities from broadcasters to writers to couturiers to heads of state come here to be feted, to lecture, to be interviewed, and to vacation. All of this makes for glamorous reading.

Other dailies from the state of Florida such as the Miami Herald with a county readership of over 8,000 or the Sun Sentinel (Fort Lauderdale) that sells even more newspapers in the south county region, seem little threat to the security of the Post. Neither do the regional papers that continue to inform their communities with area news and local advertising.

First among these is the Boca Raton News, a daily newspaper first published as a weekly on December 2, 1955. At the time Thomas F. Fleming, Jr., founder of the First Bank and Trust Company (today part of

Facing page: Like the Tropical Sun and the Palm Beach Times, Palm Beach Life magazine, a staple of island life for more than 80 years, is no more. Many new and vibrant publications, however, have risen to meet the needs of specific communities and readers throughout the county. Photo Historical Society of Palm Beach County

Nationsbank), convinced the Chamber of Commerce that Boca Raton needed a newspaper. Four years later the News had grown to twice a week, though it still largely published news of local business and civic concern. In 1969 it became a wholly-owned subsidary of Knight Newspapers (publishers of the Miami Herald), which merged to become Knight-Ridder in 1974.

The continued growth of the city caused by the establishment of Florida Atlantic University and the arrival of IBM and other major corporations, allowed the News to expand to a six-day-a-week afternoon paper and finally to add a Sunday edition and convert to a morning paper in 1986. Although the News expanded into the Delray Beach, Boynton Beach, and Deerfield Beach markets in the 1980s, it found that America's growing love affair with the quick-fix of television news, doomed the efforts to failure. To compete with readers' inability to sustain interest in a story, in 1990 the News borrowed from USA Today's format of short pointed articles, and no carry-over stories to later pages. It also reclaimed its Boca Raton News masthead and abandoned plans to become the local newspaper for all neighboring communities. All these efforts seem to have failed, and in the

The Lake Worth Herald is Lake Worth's oldest continuous business. The first issue came off the press in May, 1912 (Lake Worth was incorporated in 1913) and the newspaper continues today as the city's legal newspaper.

The Herald was started by real estate developers Bryant and Greenwood but has been under the control of the Karl J. Easton family since 1926.

Currently published by Karl J. Easton, Jr., and his two sons, Mark and Bruce, the Herald prints three sectionalized newspapers in the mid-county area of Lake Worth, Lantana, Village of Palm Springs, Lake Clarke Shores, Greenacres City, Village of Wellington and the Village of Royal Palm Beach and South Palm Beach. Photo courtesy of The Lake Worth Herald.

summer of 1997 Knight-Ridder announced that the Boca Raton News had failed to meet its expectations and was for sale.

Other local newspapers include the twice weekly Jupiter Courier, established in 1957 and purchased twenty years later by E.W. Howard (now a part of the Scripps Howard chain). Weeklies such as the Lake Worth Herald, Wellington News, and Boynton Beach News provide local color and information.

The county has two Jewish newspapers, an African-American newspaper, and two Spanish language papers. Also published in the county in Lantana is the National Enquirer. Originally brought to the Palm Beaches in 1971 by veteran newsman Generoso Pope, the tabloid flourished when Pope discovered that gore and gossip sold. With a heart as big as his circulation Pope was a generous donor to hospitals and social agencies. Since his death and sale of the paper his widow Lois Pope continues his philanthropies. The south county area has become the capital of sensationalism in the last decade where many other tabloids, including the Globe and the Star, are published.

The first radio broadcast from Palm Beach County came on February 5, 1927. Addison Mizner's boom time development company founded WFLA, "the Voice of Tropical America," to promote Boca Raton. Mizner had proposed his 1,000-watt clear channel station to broadcast "the Boca Raton message" to Florida and most of the eastern United States. He claimed that the Palm Beach Post and the New York Times had agreed to share a news hour every day between five and six o'clock. When not broadcasting news or "the facts of Florida," the station planned to play "modern adaptations of Seminole Indian music."

When Mizner first applied to the federal government for his license he found numerous barriers slowing the process between application and granting. Although test broadcasts brought reports that listeners in Canada could hear WFLA's signal, the government failed to act on the application.

By the summer of 1926 it became evident that the land boom had ended, and that Mizner's development company was in financial difficulty. In July, the Chicago-based Central Equities Corporation of Rufus Dawes and his brother, United States Vice President Charles Dawes, took over the management of the company. To have the vice president supporting the application for the radio license must have helped, as it was then quickly granted. Unfortunately, no money remained to build conventional studios. Thus the "Voice of Tropical America" broadcasted from a frame structure with its walls and roof covered with palmetto fronds. Always quick to turn adversity to virtue, the development company claimed the fronds created an acoustically superior studio. The bases of its two transmission towers can still be seen just off Palmetto Park Road on the grounds of the Boca Raton Museum of Art. Neither Mizner's development company nor the "Voice of Tropical America" survived the real estate crash.

In the early days of radio the entertainment world feared it as a serious

Palm Beach County's riches certainly add to the media. We have our own thirty radio stations and numerous "spill over" stations from adjoining counties. Finally, the choices from our own extensive television stations and our cable systems are also expanded by those from Dade and Broward counties. Photo Dave Sherman.

threat to business. But when six million people heard their first opera broardcast and hundreds of these rushed out to buy records, joy spread throughout entertainment land. Today the more than thirty Palm Beach County stations cater to individual markets such as ethnic, age, sports, diverse types of music, religion, and talk.

According to a spokesperson at WJNO regular broadcasting began there in 1939. Almost immediately in 1941 Palm Beach County received its first talk radio station, WPBR which the Aspinwalls later purchased. Palm Beachers warmly recall with nostalgia owners and talk show hosts Valerie and the late Everett Aspinwall who sold the station fifteen years later. Public broadcasting in the form of WXEL, near the top of the dial, has dedicated listeners. Primary stations are affiliated with NBC, ABC, and CBS. Owners may be local or part of the Richard Fairbanks, American Radio System, or the former Paxson consortiums.

You can take your choice among WJNO, WRMS, WJNA, WCLB, and WRLX. There is WEAT-AM and FM (news), WOLL-FM (rock and roll oldies from the 60s and 70s), WKGR-FM (Gator-classic rock), WBZT (Buzz-talk and alternative music), and WIRK (country and western). WRMB in Boynton Beach, operated by Moody Bible Institute, has no advertisers and is supported by listeners. Neither is the Spanish speaking public ignored, nor are those who find it difficult to sleep at night. All tastes and types are catered to by those voices who proselytize, analyze, and sympathize.

In 1949 television made its first appearance in Palm Beach County before reporters and Philco dealers and their wives. This first broadcast presented a local night club show. Today Palm Beach County is the 24th largest television market in the country. Its affiliates are ABC's WPBF, CBS's WFOR and WPEC, NBC's WPTV and WTVJ, and there is Ted Turner's CNN and Fox on WFLX and WSVN. The county's own channel 20 brings meetings of the Palm Beach Chamber of Commerce to the public and offers interviews with Will Ray, director of the cultural council, along with other cultural and governmental programs. Dean of the county broadcasters is William "Bill" Brooks, vice president and general manager of WPTV, he is also a Vice President of Scripps Howard Broadcasting who bought the station in 1961. The highly respected Brooks has been with the company since 1974.

Another prominent name in local television is Alex Dreyfoos Jr. former owner of WPEC. With a partner he invented a laser system that resulted in Kaiser Color Laboratories, a Photo Electronics Corporation. Dreyfoos is the hub of the cultural wheel in the county as the power behind the Palm Beach County Cultural Council and the Kravis Center, and he eagerly adds more jewels to his crown as culture king on a regular basis.

Brooks, who is more laid back, made some telling comments about television: "TV was invented to keep 'C' students employed" and "they call it the medium because it's neither rare nor well done." Brooks also tips his hat to newspapers calling them "the glue that holds the community together."

This genial executive takes issue with FCC's mandate that two hours each day must be devoted to healthy children's programming on the networks whereas cable television does as it pleases. Brooks also anticipates the arrival of digital television and believes that within a decade television sets will be equipped to receive both analog and digital TV. A spokesperson adds, "Digital will allow us to multicast, offering many more services than just television programs."

Palm Beach County is also the home of the largest broadcast television station group owner in the country. Lowell "Bud" Paxson, head of West Palm Beach's Paxson Communications, has been known as the "Infomercial King." Recently, he began buying small market and UHF television stations which no one seemed to want at the time. Now he owns, operates, or affiliates with 55 stations that have access to 56.6-million homes or 58 percent of the nation's television households. His plans seem to include a network focused on certain types of shows through selling blocks of air time rather than creating programming. In the summer of 1997 he sold all of his radio stations for $693 million and plans to use the proceeds to buy more television stations.

Palm Beach County's riches certainly extend to the media. With its wealth of local newspapers and home delivery of others such as the Miami Herald, Sun Sentinel, New York Times, and Wall Street Journal every taste and need seems covered. We have our own thirty radio stations and numerous "spill-over" stations from adjoining counties bringing such wonders as the classical programming of Miami's WTMI. Finally, the choices from our own extensive television stations and our cable systems are also expanded by those from Dade and Broward counties. Lovers of public television find this particularly fortunate. Once more, in Palm Beach County, the best of everything.

The Finer Things of Life

By Millie Wolff

A newcomer to Palm Beach County asking the question "What's new in the arts?" can expect the answer "everything," or almost everything. From the tiny community of Palm Beach has sprung a plethora of riches that has spun off in gossamer threads to the entire county. Almost everyone gives and almost everyone gets the enrichment of dance, music, theatre, and the visual arts. Big bucks and big ideas go hand in hand as witness the Kravis Center for the Performing Arts and the recently expanded Norton Museum of art.

These two big wheels located in West Palm Beach are the hubs, but around them from north to south

Through the generosity of local philanthropists and community support a plethora of cultural activities abounds in Palm Beach County. The muses have blessed the area with a rich array of dance, music, drama and the visual arts. Whatever your preference may be there is something here for everyone. Photo: The Palm Beach Post/Allen Eyeston.

Facing page: Alex W. Dreyfoos, Jr,. one of Palm Beach County's most prominent arts supporters. Chairman of the Raymond F. Kravis Center for the Performing Arts Board of Directors, Dreyfoos has been a driving force behind the cultural renaissance of Palm Beach County. He donated $1 million to Palm Beach County's High School of the Arts, which acknowledged his gift by naming the school after its most generous benefactor. Dreyfoos stands in the wings of the Kravis Center stage with members of the company of Ballet Florida. Photo C. J. Walker.

The world-class Raymond F. Kravis Center for the Performing Arts opened fully funded, with a total construction cost of $67 million, of which a remarkable $49 million came from private individuals and corporations. The Kravis Center is a success story, a prototype of a thriving performing arts center, that provides communities all over the world with an example of excellence. Photo The Kravis Center for the Performing Arts.

and west there's a lot going on. So if you elect your version of seasonal Paradise in Palm Beach, West Palm Beach, Lake Worth, Delray Beach, Boca Raton, Wellington, Jupiter, or Tequesta you can enjoy a song, a dance, a play, or a painting at a local venue or else you can make the short trek to the primary action. The chances are slim that you will be disappointed. There is little compromise on talent.

In twenty years, Palm Beach County has grown from a cultural desert into an oasis, and among those in the know, Clyde Fyfe is credited with helping turn it around. In 1978 Fyfe established the Regional Arts Foundation with funding by philanthropist Leonard D. Davis. World class musicians such as Jascha Heifitz performed in his Music at Two and Music at Eight series and brought Palm Beachers across the Lake to the acoustically deprived West Palm Beach auditorium. Out of the desire of these Palm Beachers to sponsor more cultural activities came the decision to establish an arts council.

Today William Ray is president of the Palm Beach County Cultural Council, originally known as the Palm Beach County Council for the Arts and founded by Alex W. Dreyfoos, Jr., the former president of Photo Electronics Corporation/WPEC TV-12. The inventor and philanthropist recognized the need for an organization to promote the arts in the county. In 1978 he used his television station to give public service announcements about forming an arts council and invited the public to attend a meeting. "Hordes came! We started the council that night."

The cultural council grew into an umbrella organization that helped develop the Armory Art Center, Hispanic Cultural Arts, Center for Creative Education, and Palm Beach International Film Festival. The council operates as an informational service and functions as coordinator of such endeavors as Art in Public Places; the cultural calendar; Business Committee for Culture; the Cultural Executives Committee, consisting of ninety paid members who are organization directors; and provides an arts line informational service at (800) 882-ARTS; has a volunteer staffed cultural information center at the Palm Beach International Airport; and coordinates art exhibitions for area artists inside the terminal. In 1982 county voters passed a "bed tax" in a public referendum. Many believe it succeeded because of the support of the arts council and because thirty percent of the tax went for support of the arts.

Dreyfoos, who also believed that the county needed a performing arts center to replace the inadequate and aging auditorium, immediately began raising money for the Kravis Center. While most of its $55-million cost came from private donations, then state senator Harry Johnston arranged for $10 million in public education capital outlay funds and West Palm Beach supported the center with a 1,100-car parking garage. Dreyfoos later said that the hardest part of the project was talking Raymond F. Kravis of Palm Beach into allowing his name to be used. He said that Kravis had been generous to the causes of his friends, although he had never asked them to give to his. A group of these friends, to pay him back, pledged $7 million to name the center.

The Kravis Center opened in 1992 without debt. Since then many of the world's greatest performers have come here. With the use of three halls, many local performances are also offered, such as Ballet Florida, that has received

World renown opera singer Roberta Peters, is one of many outstanding performers that appears frequently at the Kravis Center. Photo The Raymond F. Kravis Center for the Performing Arts.

The Miami Ballet has opened an office in Palm Beach and performs at the Kravis Center. Photo C. J. Walker.

Facing page: Still life photo, representing various cultural organizations of Palm Beach County. Included are dance, music, theatre and the visual arts. Photo C. J. Walker.

national recognition, as well as Palm Beach Opera, the Florida Philharmonic Orchestra, and the Broadway Series. Offerings as varied as Chinese acrobats, Marvin Hamlisch, and Jimmy Buffett have something for everyone. In 1997 the center celebrated its fifth season with 180 performances.

Among the local groups, Ballet Florida is outstanding. Marie Hale and Lynda Swaidon founded the first classical dance school in Palm Beach County in 1973. They formed the professional company in 1986 and it is one of the twenty top dance companies in the country. The facility on Fern Street has four dance studios, administrative offices, and a wardrobe department. The company consists of 21 professional dancers from all over the world. Four productions are divided among the Kravis, the Royal Poinciana Playhouse, and the Duncan Theatre of Palm Beach Community College. The Miami Ballet has also opened an office in Palm Beach and performs at the Kravis Center. Dimitri Klien Dance Company, out of Lake Worth, is Palm Beach County's contemporary dance company.

Dreyfoos, who sold Photo Electronics Corporation/WPEC-TV in 1996 for $164 million, remains one of the county's most active supporters of the arts. In 1997 he gave a one-million dollar challenge grant to the Palm Beach County School of the Arts. The school, for seventh through twelfth grade students in the communication arts, dance, music, theatre, or visual arts, must match the contribution on a two-to-one basis. In August 1997, the school moved into its newly restored eighteen-acre campus near the Kravis Center. The $28-million restoration project brought life back to the historic buildings of the former Palm Beach High School, the county's oldest.

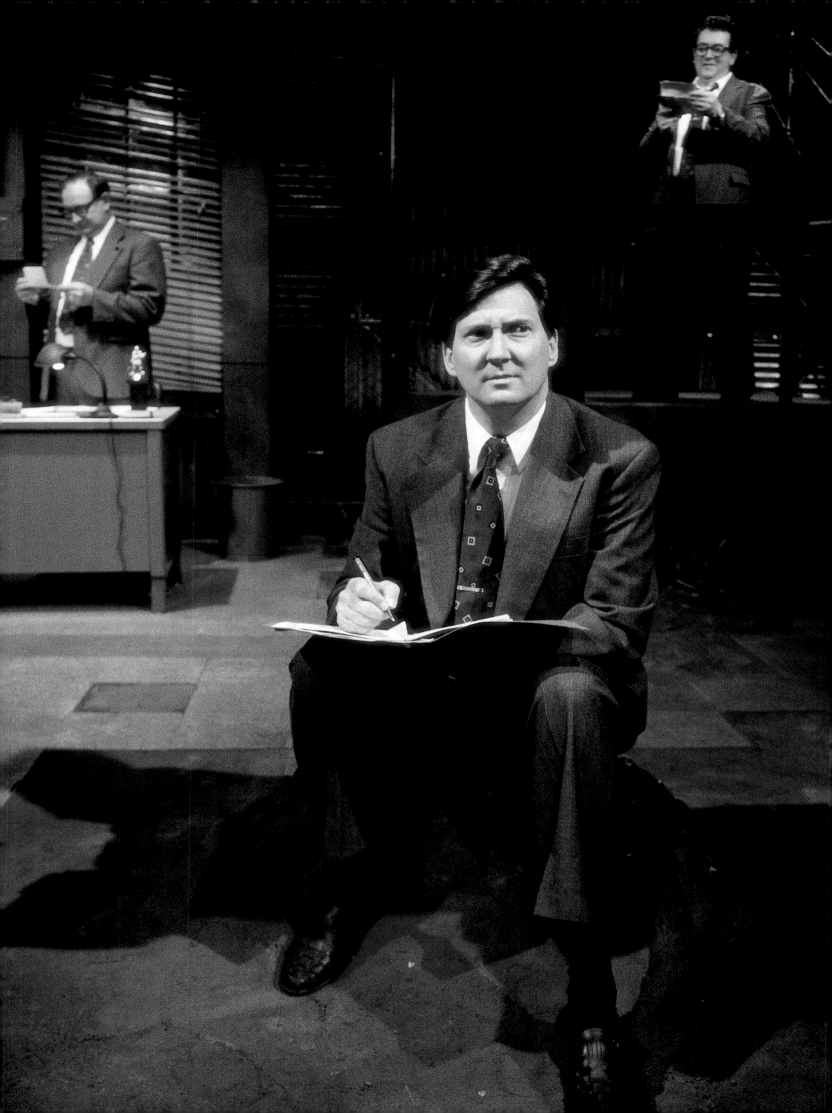

Facing page: Traber Burns, Warren Kelly, John Felix perform in "Below the Belt" by Richard Dresser, at the Pope Theatre. Photo Pope Theatre Company/Sigvision.

Top: Louis Tyrrell, Jessica K. Peterson in "Hysteria" by Terry Johnson. Photo Pope Theatre Company/Sigvision.

Left: Palm Beach Opera, "Elixir of Love." Photo Palm Beach Opera.

While fund raising for the Kravis took priority, the Norton Museum held back its plans. The original Norton Gallery and School of Art was established in 1941 by Ralph Hubbard Norton and his wife Elizabeth as a home for their outstanding art collection that grew to 500 pieces by the time Ralph Norton died in 1953. The Norton became noted for its late-nineteenth and early-twentieth century American and European paintings and is thought to have the most important jade collection east of the Mississippi River.

In 1993 board president Floyd A. Segel and director Christina Orr-Cahall launched a $23-million capital campaign. They received the support of corporations, foundations, the State of Florida, the National Endowment for the Arts, and many private donors. The new structure, completed in 1997, preserved the elements of architects Marion Sims Wyeth and William Johnson's existing historic structure. Architect Chad Floyd designed the new additions which provide a total of nineteen galleries. One of these is for exhibiting works of local artists and art associated with children's education programs. These galleries are well lighted, spacious showcases for the permanent collection and visiting shows. Ample space is provided for monumental pieces such as the Cantor collection of Rodin sculptures that celebrated the opening of the new Norton.

The Norton Museum of Art has recently completed a $23 million expansion and renovation project, more than doubling in size to 77,000 square feet — big news for what is widely agreed to be the finest art museum in Florida. Photo C. J. Walker.

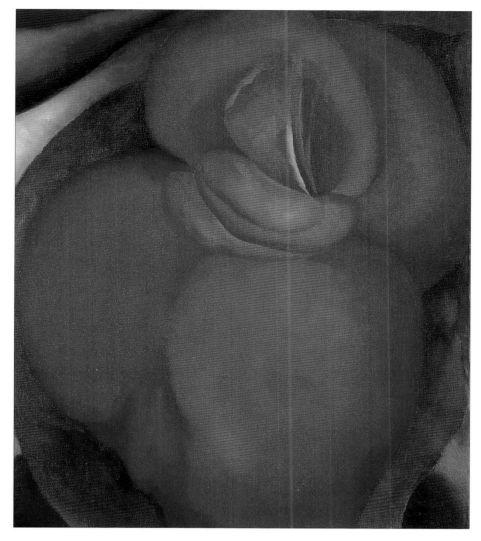

A testament to the ever-growing collection of outstanding art at the Norton, Georgia Okeeffe's the Red Flower, 1918-1919, was donated to the museum in 1996 by the Esther B. Okeeffe Charitable Foundation. Photo Norton Museum of Art.

Among the museum's most important works are Picasso's "Au Cafe," Monet's "Gardens at Bordighera," Bellows "Winter Afternoon," Pollock's "Night Mist," and "Agony in the Garden" which depicts a startling red-haired Christ, a self-portrait by Paul Gauguin. The Norton Museum of Art with its clean classical lines is truly a cultural jewel.

When the Norton tossed out the art school in 1987, the indignant students, many of them retirees, renovated the old West Palm Beach National Guard Armory built in 1939 as a WPA project from the Art Moderne designs of architect William Manley King. The building served as the local headquarters of the Florida National Guard until 1982 and then stood vacant and deteriorating until the art students arrived. The Armory, partially restored through grants for historic preservation from the State of Florida, now serves as the home of art classes, exhibitions, and special events. Almost in view of the Kravis Center, the Armory has proved a panacea for artists who had no place to go.

Although the Kravis Center and the Norton Museum may be the "big two" around which other county cultural organizations revolve, there are many other institutions worthy of mention. Palm Beach's Royal Poinciana Playhouse, established in the thirties, brought some of the earliest theatri-

cal productions to the county. A platform for traveling road shows employing the star system, the Playhouse became famous for opening nights when the high society ladies turned out in their designer gowns and precious jewels to light up the lives of onlookers as they strode down the red carpet from limousines to the theatre entrance. Camera bulbs flashed to record this affluence for the *Palm Beach Daily News.* With cocktail parties before curtain time, audiences sometimes snoozed, often left at intermission, or walked out on curtain calls. Actors from Broadway to Kalamazoo considered Palm Beach audiences cold and abominably rude.

In the early 1920s, the Society of Arts, under the direction of Joseph Riter and Hugh Dillman, sponsored musical programs such as the Cleveland Symphony Orchestra at the Paramount Theatre and art exhibits at Whitehall, the former Flagler mansion. In 1934 Maud Howe Elliot spearheaded a movement to promote interest in art, literature, music, and science and to found a library and art museum. The Society of the Four Arts, chartered in February 1936, held its first exhibit of fifty old-master paintings, borrowed mainly from Palm Beach collectors, in an empty store room in what became the Embassy Apartments on Royal Palm Way. In 1937 architect Maurice Fatio, a member of the society's board, designed the library. An early and close relationship between the Society and the Garden Club of Palm Beach led to the gardens on the library's grounds. In 1947 the society purchased Colonel E.R. Bradley's Embassy Club and architect John L. Volk created a 1,000-seat auditorium from its patio, and galleries in other sections of the building. Finally, in the 1990s, the Society added the Embassy Apartments, where it had held its first exhibit, to its complex.

An exclusive membership of Old Guard families continues with new members who are often legacies. Nonetheless, anyone may purchase tickets to events unless, because of the small size of the auditorium, they are restricted to members. Guest lecturers have included Hedrick Smith, Art Buchwald, Mark Shields, Lady Margaret Thatcher, and Prince Philip. Four seasonal musical programs have included groups such as the Brzoni String Quartet and the Montreal Symphony. Quality films are shown on Fridays and films relating to current gallery exhibitions are shown on Sundays. Artistic programs for young people are presented several times a year.

For the 58th season in 1996, an annual juried national exhibition of contemporary American painting drew artists from fifty states. The other exhibits included "Mingei: Japanese Folk Art from the Montgomery Collection," "Two Hundred Years of English Naive Art (1700-1900)," and "The Spirit of Montmarte: Cabarets, Humor, and the Avant-Garde (1875-1905)." Although the Society of the Four Arts is seasonal, and galleries are open to the public only from December to April, the library is open for the entire year and any resident may purchase a library card.

The Ann Weaver Norton Sculpture Gardens with its monumental brick and granite sculptures by the late Ann Norton is one of several

The Anne Norton Sculpture Gardens with its monumental brick and granite sculptures. Photo Dave Sherman.

Facing page: Pan's Garden is designed to attract passing birds and butterflies. Photo Dave Sherman.

Although the Society of the Four Arts is seasonal these splendid outdoor murals can be viewed all year. Photo Tony Arruza

These outdoor murals depict Greek mythological muses that symbolize the four arts: music, drama, art and literature. Photo Dave Sherman.

gardens in the county open to the public. In Palm Beach, the Preservation Foundation's Pan's Garden (sculptor Frederick MacMonnies's 1890 statue, "Pan of Rohallion" is set in a pool at its entrance) uses native upland and wetland plants in natural settings. The garden is designed to attract passing birds and butterflies and to require a minimum of human care. Architect Leslie Divoll designed the two garden pavilions which serve as offices and open class rooms. Mounts Botanical Garden in West Palm Beach also grows species indigenous to Florida.

As one travels south to Lake Worth, the Palm Beach Community College Museum of Art, a 1989 gift of the Lannan Foundation, which also donated its entire collection of glass, ceramics, and kinetics, features contemporary art. J. Patrick Lannan, the late chairman of ITT had founded the museum in a former movie theatre to house his collection of contemporary art. The college has continued this tradition by sponsoring exhibits of art so far out that one in early 1997 was titled "Is it Art?"

The community college's Duncan Theatre on the central campus offers a variety of programs including the Ballet Nacional De Carcas, Aman Folk Ensemble, Stuttgart Chamber Orchestra, and Jazz Dance. Two other community college theatres, the Dolly Hand Cultural Arts Center in Belle Glade and one on the Palm Beach Gardens campus also provide a number of theatrical and musical events for their communities.

South of Lake Worth is Manalapan with its 285-seat Lois Pope Theatre. Louis Tyrell's challenging programming has produced some of the county's most exciting theatre. The play "Lonely Planet" dealt with friendship and tolerance in the age of AIDS, while "The Killing of Michael Malloy," was a comedy about murder for profit. The Lois Pope Foundation helps pay the bills with an annual grant of $250,000. Since its first season in 1987, the box office has also done well.

One of Palm Beach County's most impressive cultural institutions tends to be a "hidden treasure." The Morikami Museum and Japanese Gardens in western Delray Beach combines a museum of Japanese culture; a Japanese house museum with a permanent exhibition on Yamato, the early Japanese colony in Boca Raton; and a five-acre Japanese garden, all within a 150-acre park.

In 1904 the first settlers arrived at Jo Sakai's farming colony of Yamato (meaning large peaceful country, an ancient name for Japan) in northern Boca Raton. Although the colony failed to survive, several of the settlers remained in the area and prospered. One of these, George Sukeji Morikami, through years of hard work built a fortune in land west of Delray Beach. He received American citizenship in 1967 at the age of 82, and decided to repay his adopted country by giving Palm Beach County the park that today bears his name.

Starting with the Japanese house and its small garden, under the direction of Larry Rosensweig, the institution has added a large museum and greatly expanded gardens. The museum has a 225-seat auditorium for lectures and a Japanese cafe serving lunch. Traveling exhibits, classes in calligraphy, the tea ceremony ritual, the growing of Bonsai, combined with traditional Japanese celebrations such as the Bon Festival, Oshogatsu (New Year's 'party'), and the Hatsume Fair (Spring Festival), bring thousands of visitors to the museum.

In Boca Raton, Florida Atlantic University's Department of Theatre offered its first production, "Last Letters from Stalingrad" under the direction of Joseph Conaway at Marymount College in 1965. Its season since then, whether in the main theatre, the small studio theatre, or the new "black box" has brought south Florida residents everything from Shakespeare to Broadway musicals to new experimental plays. The Dorothy F. Schmidt Chair has been held by theatre legend Joshua Logan, who directed the world premier of his play "Huck and Jim on the

Traditional Japanese celebrations such as the Bon festival, Oshogatsu (New Year's 'party'), and the Hatsume Fair (Spring Festival), bring thousands of visitors to The Morikami Museum and Japanese Gardens. Photo Dave Sherman.

Mississippi" at the university, playwright Edward Albee, and actors Hume Cronyn and Tony Award winner Zoe Caldwell. The Ritter and Schmidt art galleries maintain full exhibition schedules during the academic year and the Florida Philharmonic performs its Boca Raton concerts in the university's 2,400-seat auditorium.

In the mid-1980s, Boca Raton residents began hearing about "Art Park," a concept of Jamie Snyder and the Community Redevelopment Agency to replace the aging Boca Raton Mall with a cultural center containing theatres, concert halls, and science and art museums, partially supported by shops, restaurants, offices, and apartments. When Mizner Park opened in the early 1990s, the cultural institutions were conspicuous by their absence. Although both the Caldwell Theatre and the Boca Raton Museum of Art had planned new facilities in the center, they backed out when the economic climate seemed to preclude the type of fund raising necessary for their projects.

The International Museum of Cartoon Art became the first cultural institution to settle amongst Mizner Park's high scale restaurants and retail stores. Established in New York by cartoonist Mort Walker, the museum's extensive permanent collection is enhanced by major visiting exhibits such as "Remembering the Magic! A Celebration of Walt Disney World," to commemorate its 25th anniversary, and the political cartoons of the *Miami Herald's* Jim Morin.

Over the years, other cultural institutions realized their missed opportunities and in the summer of 1997 a new umbrella group, Concert Hall at Mizner Park (or CHAMP), proposed to develop the almost six-acres at Mizner Park's north end. Architects envision a 1,800-seat concert hall for the Florida Philharmonic and the Boca Raton Pops, and a new Boca Raton Museum of Art, wrapped around a "Concert Green" defined by a two story horseshoe-shaped cloister. Once again, retail and office space, restaurants, and apartments were proposed to help pay for the cultural space. The museum and both musical organizations have agreed to move to Mizner Park. Although the value of the project seemed obvious, the usual "nay sayers" gathered their supporters and began preaching impending doom.

All essays have a beginning and an end. They also have a limit. But we remind the readers of the Hibel Museum of Art in Palm Beach, "the world's only nonprofit public museum dedicated to the art of a living woman;" the South Florida Science Museum, where you can see stars that do not sing or dance but do twinkle; the Palm Beach Zoo at Dreher Park; Palm Beach Photographic Centre in Delray Beach; the gardens at the Episcopal Church of Bethesda-by-the-Sea in Palm Beach; the Henry Morrison Flagler Museum; the Jewish Community Centers; Jan McArt's Royal Palm Dinner Theatre; Delray Beach's Old School Square; and the Lighthouse Gallery and School of Art in Tequesta. Are these cultural institutions important? According to a study by William B. Stronge and Aileen D. Maale, the total economic impact of these organizations in 1994 was over three-quarters-billion dollars and they supplied over 15,000 jobs.

Left: Crest Theatre, (interior restored) origi-nally the Delray High School, this 320-seat state-of-the-art facility features professional dance, music and theatre throughout the year. Photo Dan Fore.

The Crest Theatre interior prior to restora-tion. Photo Old School Square/Crest Theatre.

Left: Crest Theatre former 1925 high school after restoration. The Theatre is located in the Old School Square Historic District in Delray Beach. Photo Old School Square/Crest Theatre.

When Whitehall was completed in 1902, the New York Herald proclaimed it the "Taj Mahal of North America." Architects John Carrére and Thomas Hastings designed the 60,000-square-foot, 55 room Gilded Age estate in Palm Beach for Henry M. Flagler. Carrére and Hastings were trained at the Ecole des Beaux-arts in Paris and also designed the New York Public Library, the Frick Estate in New York City, and the U.S. Senate and House of Representatives Office Buildings in Washington, D.C. Today, Whitehall is an historic house museum listed on the National Register of Historic Places and open to the public as the

Henry Morrison Flagler Museum. Visitors to the Flagler Museum learn about America's Gilded Age and Flagler's contribution to Florida's development. Henry Flagler, with partners John D. Rockefeller and Samuel Andrews, founded Standard Oil in 1870. However, around the turn-of-the-century, Flagler's interests turned to the development of Florida. Flagler's Florida East Coast Railway, and the luxury hotels he built along the way, linked the entire east coast of Florida, establishing agriculture and tourism as Florida's top industries and Palm Beach as one of the world's great winter resorts.

Flagler's private railcar is displayed on the South Lawn of the Museum. Throughout the year, the Flagler Museum mounts exhibits related to America's Gilded Age, the life of Henry Flagler and the history of Florida.

Photos clockwise top left: exterior of the Henry M. Flagler Museum, The Louis XIV Music Room, The Marble Hall and the Dining Room. Photos The Henry M. Flagler Museum.

The Good Life

By Barbara Marshall

P alm Beach was founded in Gilded Age excess and has never strayed from its lavish roots. At the turn of the century, the resort town that bequeathed its name to Palm Beach County, was a luxurious rest stop for newly-minted American millionaires. Henry Flagler's 1902 Beaux Arts mansion, Whitehall, now the Henry Morrison Flagler Museum, remains as a stunning souvenir of Gilded Age grandeur.

But the rich weren't the only ones lured by a place where "summer spends the winter." Up and down the coastline and along the shores of Lake Okeechobee, new towns sprung up founded by people seeking new lives in America's last wilderness — West Palm Beach,

The most spectacular remaining castle is Mar-a-Largo, Marjorie Merriweather Post's 1927 Venetian-Moorish-Mediterranean fantasy, now a private club owned by developer, Donald Trump. Trump renovated the dining room adding small intimate tables, replacing Mrs. Post's huge marble rectangular table, upon which presidents and kings had wined and dined. Photo C. J. Walker.

Lake Worth, Delray Beach, Boca Raton. Further west, the rich soil of Belle Glade attracted farmers as astonishing quantities of Lake Okeechobee catfish were hooking commercial fisherman.

By the early 1920s, Palm Beach County was an unlikely but vibrant mix of wintering social register families, plucky pioneer farmers, and brash business people, all seeking their individual versions of "The Good Life" in a balmy, palmy paradise. Their descendants and thousands of others — urbanites, small town residents, snowbirds, socialites, immigrants from Latin America and the Caribbean, and refugees from the cold and dreary north — are seeking it still.

The Roaring Twenties, the razzmatazz Jazz Age, gave Palm Beach its reputation as the sandbox of the swells. Newly-built mansions by society architects such as Addison Mizner and Maurice Fatio became repositories for all that glittered, vacuumed up by the unfettered consumption of the times, and spit out on the sandy shores of paradise.

The most spectacular remaining castle is Mar-a-Lago, Marjorie Merriweather Post's 1927 Venetian-Moorish-Mediterranean fantasy, now a private club owned by developer, Donald Trump. For a $75,000 initiation fee and room rate of $1,000 a night, members can stay in one of several themed bedrooms, such as the Spanish room or the Adam room, in which Mrs. Post once ensconced presidents and kings.

Worth Avenue: One of the world's most famous and beautiful shopping streets where kings and queens walk unnoticed amongst the cosmopolitan shopper. Top photo Tony Arruza. Right photo Palm Beach County Convention & Visitors Bureau.

Palm Beach is still home to the super rich who continue to build staggeringly large manses. The island's newest real estate trend is the Palm Beach version of urban renewal — tearing down older, non-landmarked mansions to build mega-mansions in excess of 30,000 square feet, palatial temples to "The Good Life." Well-heeled buyers have paid millions — as much as $11 million, in one notable case — for a house they plan to immediately raze to build something even bigger and much more grand.

Elsewhere charity may be a virtue but it's a vocation in Palm Beach. During the season, the international social elite flocks to the island's charity balls, galas, and luncheons which raise millions of dollars to fight disease and aid the needy. The Red Cross Ball, which began in 1937 and recently raised $750,000, and the Valentines' Day Heart Ball, the traditional twin peaks of the social season, are feeling the challenge from the newer and increasingly more social Preservation Foundation Ball. Palm Beachers were also largely responsible, along with local government contributions, for donations which allowed the multi-million dollar Raymond J. Kravis Center for the Performing Arts to open debt-free.

Charity events also provide occasions for Palm Beachers to wear the couture clothes sold in the exclusive shops on Worth Avenue, one of the world's most famous and beautiful shopping streets. Worth Avenue merchants once described their street as the place "where kings and queens walk unnoticed amongst the common shoppers." Today, the celebrities dashing into Tiffany, Gucci, Valentino, Van Cleef & Arpels, Armani, or Hermes are as likely to be famous television talk show hosts, sports figures, or rock stars.

Boca Raton's Mizner Park is a popular meeting place that looks and feels like an upscale village within-the-city. Shops, restaurants, movie theatres, and an amphitheatre provide a family-friendly mix of activities, including a variety of free concerts. Photo Palm Beach County Convention & Visitors Bureau.

A canoe trip along the Loxahatchee River winds through a sub-tropical forest of hundred year old cypress. Photo Tony Arruza.

In parts of Palm Beach County, a Florida remains that is slipping rapidly away elsewhere in the state. You can find it in the wild, quiet places, such as the Arthur R. Marshall Loxahatchee National Wildlife Refuge, one of the last northeastern vestiges of the Everglades, where you can look out over the kind of sawgrass prairie that once covered the southern end of Florida with a River of Grass. You'll find it during a canoe trip along the Northwest Fork of the Loxahatchee River, a federally designated

Arthur R. Marshall Loxahatchee National Wildlife Refuge, where one can look over a sawgrass prairie that once covered the southern end of Florida with a River of Grass. Photo Dave Sherman.

Wild and Scenic River, which winds through a tangled sub-tropical forest of hundred year old cypress. You might discover a slice of real Florida during a summer's day at DuBois Park in Jupiter or during a stroll through Lake Worth's period piece of a downtown. Even the Palm Beach Bike Path, which follows the curve of Lake Worth north to the Palm Beach Inlet as it passes lakefront mansions, allows a view of Old Florida when it reaches the old shingled Bethesda-by-the-Sea Church, now a private residence.

Photo Tony Arruza

Photo courtesy PBC

Geography and climate determined Palm Beach County's destiny. Riding a bulge of land that sticks eastward into the Atlantic Ocean, the county is closer to the Gulfstream than anywhere else in Florida. That proximity accounts for the remarkably clear, deep blue color of the Atlantic along the county's 47 miles of coastline, which contain some of the state's most distinctive beaches: snorkelers' favorite Red Reef Park in Boca Raton; the palm-lined municipal beach at Delray Beach; pristine John D. MacArthur State Park, and Juno Beach, popular with surfers.

The northward flow of the stream brings game fish close to shore and nourishes natural and artificial offshore reefs, as well as a thriving dive industry. Divers visiting reefs and offshore wrecks frequently find themselves swimming with sea turtles, which lay their eggs on local beaches during the summer nesting season. During winter cold spells, hundreds of huge docile manatees congregate in Intracoastal canals and in the warm water near FPL's Riviera Beach power plant.

Outsiders tend to think of the rest of Palm Beach County as an upscale extension of Palm Beach, but the reality is that this county, larger than the state of Delaware, is a dizzying clutch of lifestyles, cultures and neighbor-hoods — wealthy, middle-class and poverty-stricken. The county changes its countenance in each of its cities, from neighborly small towns to sophis-ticated urban centers. On the edge of Lake Okeechobee, the county's "other coast," the good and bad of Old Florida hangs on tenaciously. Communities, such as Canal Point and Lake Harbor, evoke the quaint homespun atmosphere of past decades. In the farming towns of Belle Glade, Pahokee, and South Bay, the quaint charm is tempered by alarming pockets of poverty and neglect.

Although there is a homogenizing sameness to the strip shopping mall, fast food joint-lined main roads, many of the county's cities have main-tained — or are recapturing — the charming sense of place that once made them unique. There is a new appreciation of the area's history, evident in the old downtowns undergoing revitalization and historic neighborhoods which are attracting young families, all barely imaginable a decade ago.

Photo courtesy PBC-CVB

Photo Tony Arruza

The new Centennial Fountain that Governor Lawton Chiles and West Palm Beach mayor, Nancy Graham, christened with an inaugural stroll through it. Photo City of West Palm Beach.

West Palm Beach entered a new era on its 100th birthday by recapturing its historic past. On that fall night in 1994, Governor Lawton Chiles grabbed the arm of West Palm Beach mayor, Nancy Graham, and christened the new Centennial Fountain with an inaugural stroll through it. It may have ruined Chiles' trademark cowboy boots, but it signaled a new life for the once-decrepit and abandoned downtown of the county's biggest city.

The revitalization of Clematis, the city's main street, is a cornerstone of the rebirth of downtown West Palm Beach. The blocks of once vacant store fronts are now an entertainment district with trendy bars and outdoor cafes. The new waterfront Meyer Amphitheater is the site of frequent free concerts. Weekends kick off early in West Palm Beach with Thursday's Clematis By Night weekly street party, when the streets are jammed with families, young professionals, and seniors enjoying the Centennial fountain, free music, and the camaraderie of friends and neighbors.

West Palm Beach residents have embraced historic preservation so enthusiastically that the city has established twelve historic neighborhoods. During annual historic home tours, residents invite the public to admire their restored residences and stabilized neighborhoods.

The city has embarked on an unprecedented $375 million downtown redevelopment project called CityPlace, being built on 77 acres east of the Kravis Center for the Performing Arts. In cooperation with the city, Boston-based developer Ken Himmel is constructing retail and office space, a large hotel, entertainment venues, and residential units on land left vacant by the failed Downtown/Uptown redevelopment project. City, county, and state government agencies are discussing funding for a future convention center adjacent to CityPlace.

Delray Beach, an All-American City and a Florida Main Street Community, is also preparing for the future by embracing the legacy of its past. The city has lovingly preserved its old-fashioned downtown, a mix of restaurants, nightclubs, art galleries, antiques shops, and the historic Colony hotel all within a few blocks of one of the county's best public beaches. The popular monthly Art and Jazz on the Avenue events brings thousands downtown to hear free music and visit shops, which stay open late.

In Boca Raton, Mizner Park is a popular meeting place that looks and feels like an upscale village-within-the-city. Shops, restaurants, movie theaters, and an amphitheater provide a family-friendly mix of activities, including a variety of free concerts. Addison Mizner, the architect who created the Mediterranean look of Palm Beach, also left his imprint on Boca Raton. Mizner designed the Boca Raton Resort and Club and many of the homes in the historic Old Floresta neighborhood, during the boom years of the 1920s.

Sports have been a major component of the good life here since the days when beach censors determined whether a woman's swimming costume was demure enough for public viewing. Then, swimming and golf

CityPlace is a new development scheduled to break ground in 1998, that promises to be one of the most exciting and unique mixed-use projects in the country. Including speciality retail, restaurant, cinema, live theater, hotel, office and residential uses, CityPlace will offer over 600,000 sq. ft. of leasable retail space organized around cultural and entertainment activities. The physical heart of the project is "Church Plaza", a pedestrian-friendly open air square. This activity intensive plaza is anchored by a landmark former church structure to be transformed into a performance hall. The street front environment will be further enhanced by on-street parking, individualized retail storefronts, outdoor dining in 12 distinctive destination restaurants and extensive use of arcade, loggia, landscape and water features. CityPlace renderings courtesy City of West Palm Beach.

were the popular sports. They still are today, along with many more.

Home of the Professional Golfers' Association, Palm Beach County has more than 145 golf courses, more than any other county in the United States. The PGA complex, in Palm Beach Gardens, has hosted many of the world's top tournaments, such as the PGA Seniors' Championship and the Ladies Professional Golf Association. Thousands of fans come out to watch local residents Jack Nicklaus, Greg Norman, and Michelle McGann when they play their home courses.

The fact that tennis legend, Chris Evert, lives in Boca Raton and the existence of more than 1,100 tennis courts testify to the popularity of the sport in Palm Beach County.

For 35 years, baseball fans have reveled in the rites of spring training at the West Palm Beach baseball stadium, which is being replaced by a new $28-million, 7,000-seat stadium in Jupiter's Abacoa community. The stadium, which will open for the 1998 season, will be the new spring training home for the St. Louis Cardinals and the Montreal Expos. Various private and government agencies are discussing plans for construction of a new sports arena for the county, which will take the place of the West Palm Beach Auditorium.

While deep water docks are a status symbol to eastern Palm Beach County residents, horse stalls are the upscale *accouterment* for those who live in the western suburbs. The Village of Wellington is the county's equestrian center, home of the posh Palm Beach Polo and Country Club, and winter home for the international polo, show jumping, and dressage circuit. Polo fans gather for champagne-and-caviar tailgate parties at the Palm Beach Polo grounds during the winter, as well as at the Royal Palm Sports Club in Boca Raton and Gulfstream Polo Club in Lake Worth, also the site of the National Museum of Polo and Hall of Fame. Wellington is also the headquarters of the United States Croquet Association.

For some, the good life means unabashed luxury, which is defined three ways in Palm Beach County: The Breakers, The Four Seasons Resort, and the Ritz-Carlton in Manalapan, all AAA Five-Diamond Resorts. The *grande dame* of the hotels is The Breakers in Palm Beach which completed a $75 million renovation in 1997. Formal afternoon tea service is popular at several Palm Beach hotels, including the Ritz-Carlton and the Chesterfield.

The county's culinary scene has matured in recent years and now boasts more than 2,000 restaurants, from rustic ethnic eateries to exquisite and expensive temples of *haute* cuisine. There are cosmopolitan bistros, waterfront seafood bars, even Cafe Protégé, a restaurant run by the master chefs and students at the prestigious Florida Culinary Institute. In Boca Raton, baseball fans can watch Pete Rose broadcast his radio show from the Pete Rose Ballpark Cafe, a combination restaurant, sports bar, and entertainment complex. La Vielle Maison, also in Boca Raton, is ranked as one of the top restaurants in the country by Zagat's and Mobile Travel Guide.

Thousands of fans come out to watch local favorites, Jack Nicklaus and Chris Evert. Top photo The Palm Beach Post/Sherman Zent. Lower photo C. J. Walker.
Facing page: Polo the sport of kings. Photo courtesy Gulfstream Polo Club/David Lominska.

Croquet is taken very seriously in Palm Beach County. The national croquet championship is played here each year and Palm Beach Gardens is the home of the United States Croquet Association. Photo Palm Beach County Convention & Visitors Bureau.

In Palm Beach, Bice is a favorite restaurant of the see-and-be-seen social crowd, while younger islanders visit Amici for dining and dancing. Testa's has been a Palm Beach fixture since the 1920s and Ta-boo, a world-class American Bistro and Bar, represents the true meaning of the word éclat.

In West Palm Beach, a young and trendy crowd hops from bar to restaurant to nightspot along Clematis Street. On Thursday nights, sunset at the Sailfish Marina brings crowds to the Singer Island marina and restaurant for fresh seafood and a weekly arts and crafts show. However, the real show is the astonishing display of fish visible in the marina's clear waters, which is near the mouth of the Palm Beach Inlet.

From fall to spring, people gather early on Saturday mornings at Greenmarkets in West Palm Beach, Delray Beach, and Jupiter. A Cuban coffee stand serves thick and sweet *cafe con leche* to shoppers who breakfast on free samples of just-baked breads, fruit, jams and jellies, and locally-made goat cheese while filling bags with organic vegetables and local exotic flowers.

Nearly every weekend, there is a festival of some kind in Palm Beach County. The largest and most famous is SunFest, which celebrated its fifteenth year in May 1997. Spread along the serpentine waterfront of West Palm Beach, the festival is a five-day extravaganza of top-name musical talent, a juried art show, and a mammoth fireworks display.

Other annual festivals and events include the West Palm Beach Boat Show, a major "in-the-water" show; Palm Beach Gardens' Artigras, one of south Florida's biggest fine arts festivals; the Japanese New Year Celebration at the Morikami Museum and Japanese Gardens in Delray Beach; and FotoFusion, seminars and exhibits by some of the world's leading photographers. Boynton Beach's G.A.L.A., the Delray Affair (a legacy of the annual spring gladioli festival), and the "Meet Me Downtown" festival in Boca Raton bring thousands to these downtown arts and crafts festivals.

Proof that Palm Beach County is no longer just a haven for wealthy retirees is the proliferation of activities for children. The Dreher Park Zoo is undergoing a major renovation and expansion while Lion Country Safari allows visitors to drive through the habitats of elephants, giraffes, and naturally, lions. The Rapids Water Park is a river of good, clean fun while the South Florida Science Museum and the Children's Science Explorium in Boca Raton provide hands-on learning experiences. Themed, community-built playgrounds in Lake Worth, Boca Raton, Delray Beach, and West Palm Beach, are a demonstration of the area's increasing commitment to children's needs.

It's difficult to grasp the staggering diversity of Palm Beach County, one of the largest counties east of the Mississippi River. One might imagine looking at it through a kaleidoscope, where one image is refracted into dozens of separate views, each slightly different, but all a necessary part of the whole.

This kaleidoscope might reveal a bass boat slicing through the flat water of Lake Okeechobee. A Palm Beach woman in a couture gown greeting dinner party guests. Children dancing through Centennial Fountain in downtown West Palm Beach. In Wellington, a teenage girl carefully guiding her horse around her backyard riding ring. Men drinking *cafe cubano,* arguing politics in rapid-fire Spanish, and gesturing emphatically across a coffee shop counter. In a country club neighborhood, the laughter of a group of winter residents gathered for poolside cocktails floats over their community golf course. The spicy-sweet smell of barbecued pork vies for attention with the sound of a reggae band in an urban park.

Over it all, uniting the images and knitting them together, arches a vast sub-tropical sky, which curves low into the gray shallows of Lake Okeechobee on one side, and on the other, into the limitless blue-green ocean.

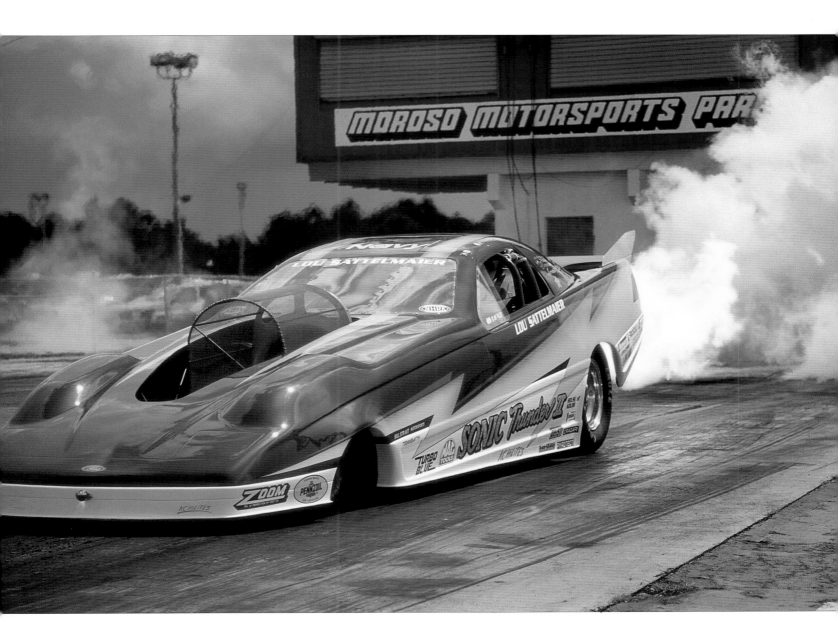

It is difficult to grasp the staggering diversity of Palm Beach County. One might imagine looking at it through a kaleidoscope, where one image is refracted into dozens of separate views, each slightly different, but all a necessary part of the whole. Facing page Ferris Wheel, photo C. J. Walker. Flower shopping in Greenmarket, photo the City of West Palm beach. Photos this page Palm Beach County Sports Commission.

Photos clockwise top left: Palm Beach Horticultural Society's Tropical Flower Show, where creative designs, and colorful ideas abound. Photo C. J. Walker.

Uncle Sam, a July 4, favorite. Photo The Palm Beach Post/Lannis Waters.

Christmas in south Florida, with festive decorations and traditional dress. Photo The Palm Beach Post/Greene.

Palm Beach County's multi ethnic community celebrates Black Awareness Day. Photo The Palm Beach Post/Caroline Couig.

Exotic flora, like the red hibiscus, can be found in bloom all year long in southeast Florida. Photo Palm Beach County Convention & Visitors Bureau.

The Palm Beach Zoo at Dreher Park is under-going extensive renovation and complete modernization. The new zoo will include one of the largest tropical rainforest exhibits in the nation. At the zoo, some 300,500 annual visitors, including 37,500 school-children enjoy more than 400 animals on 23 acres of outdoor exhibits year round. Historically, zoos were little more than menageries, collections of a variety of animals. Visitors marveled at how big or small or colorful or oddly shaped each animal was. Zoological parks here in the U.S. began to show that all of these unique features of animals — their long necks, a bird's unusually shaped bill, a cat's agility and ability to hunt — were uniquely suited to life in a particular kind of habitat. All of these habitats that support unique animals, support people too. They all represent the extraordinary natural, living resources on which we — our human species, depends. Photos Palm Beach Zoo at Dreher Park/Dave Sherman.

Top right: Lion Country Safari, allows visitors to drive through the habitats of Elephants, Giraffes, and of course Lions. Photo Dave Sherman.

Almost every weekend there is a festival of some kind in Palm Beach County. The largest and most famous is SunFest. Top photo C. J. Walker. Photo right SunFest.

Facing page: The Okeechobee Cattleman's Rodeo. In parts of Palm Beach County a Florida remains that is slipping rapidly away elsewhere in the state. Photo The Palm Beach Post/Paul Milette.

From Flagler to "The Best of Everything"

By Stuart B. McIver

Before Flagler the island had coconut palms, sandy beaches, one small hotel and little else except for the most important ingredient of all — superb weather. Sunshine, just the right amount; balmy breezes, and in the winter when icy winds rake the north, not too much rain.

In less than a decade after Henry Morrison Flagler discovered Palm Beach in 1892 the Great Man had transformed the island into America's premier winter resort, the watering hole of the socially elite. For his rich and famous clientele he built the world's largest wooden resort hotel, the 1,150–room Royal Poinciana, gazing out on the waters of Lake Worth, and the

The Flagler Era established the Palm Beaches as an international tourist destination, enhancing the area's natural attractions with the stylish allure of such landmarks as The Breakers hotel. The Breakers provides legendary golf on a unique ocean-front course, along with fourteen immaculately maintained tennis courts.

Photo The Breakers.

Palm Beach Inn (later renamed The Breakers), smaller but every bit as luxurious, facing the Atlantic Ocean. He provided formal teas in the Cocoanut Grove and elegant dining in a hall so big author Ring Lardner once wrote it was "a toll call" from one end of the room to the other. Both the beach and the weather came with the territory, offering guests ocean bathing and boating. For entertainment Flagler supplied orchestras for listening and dancing, a golf course and winter baseball of major league caliber. High-stakes gamblers found Colonel E.R. Bradley's Beach Club, the country's most exclusive and formal casino, within walking distance of the Royal Poinciana, or the Ponce as the regulars called it. From his newly created town of Westpalmbeach, which he originally spelled as one word, Flagler drew help for a wide variety of service jobs.

To make it easy for winter visitors to reach his new resort, he extended his Florida East Coast Railway south to Westpalmbeach on the western shore of Lake Worth. A separate spur carried the cream of American society across the water to Palm Beach.

That left just one more building block to assure the creation of a great resort. Flagler had put together lodgings, dining, entertainment, sports and

Mary Lily Flagler served tea on the Whitehall lawn for a fashionably dressed party. Her sister Jesse Kenan Wise is third from the right and her sister-in-law Alice Pomeroy Kenan, who married William Rand Kenan is third from the left. Photo Henry Morrison Flagler Museum Archives.

convenient transportation. Now he needed to make sure that his potential paying customers knew where and what Palm Beach was. The Flagler interests, a far-flung empire which included his railroad, resort hotels, steamships, newspapers and a large land development company, had already acquired advertising and publicity skills. An elaborate color brochure declared: "Palm Beach is one of the most beautiful sections of all Florida. Its wonderful winter climate, its great natural charm, and its two sumptuous hotels make it the greatest winter resort in this or any other country.

Social activity is at its height during the Palm Beach season and there is a continuous series of amusements and gayety. In the superb climate society spends most of its time out-of-doors. Tea on the lawn at the Royal Poinciana is a social feature of the day, and golf, tennis, surf-bathing, or the plunge in the pool are among the daily recreations. There are no horses or automobiles at Palm Beach, and the only vehicle outside of the wheel chair, is a little mule-power tram-car, running between The Breakers and the Royal Poinciana.

The Breakers is on the opposite side of Palm Beach, facing the ocean. It is connected with Lake Worth and the Royal Poinciana by a magnificent Avenue of Palms....and between the hours of eleven and one o'clock the spacious piazzas of The Breakers are crowded with the gayest of Palm Beach throngs, gathered to hear the music of the combined orchestras of both hotels, and to witness society on noon parade."

Travel writers were invited to see for themselves. Wrote a Philadelphia Press travel editor in January, 1895: "On Monday of this week nearly 100 men and women were in the surf here bathing at one time. On the same day, the average temperature in Philadelphia was 26 degrees. This will give

The afternoon tea dance in the Cocoanut Grove became a daily ritual for the guests of Flagler's hotels. A society orchestra provided music for dancing in the vast garden off the southwest corner of the Royal Poinciana hotel. The fashionably attired woman often changed costumes seven times during a single day at the resort. Beginning with breakfast in the dining room, continuing with morning on the beach, lunch, afternoon sightseeing, the tea dance, and ending with the finest jewels and best gowns for dinner and more dancing. Photo Henry Morrison Flagler Museum Archives.

a good idea of the difference of living in Philadelphia and in Palm Beach."

The Flagler Era established the Palm Beaches as an international tourist destination. West Palm Beach opened itself up into three words and in addition opened itself up to the stream of tourists who were learning about the wonders of Florida. At a 1913 meeting of the West Palm Beach of Trade, forerunner to the West Palm Beach Chamber of Commerce, members hammered out an agreement to print an advertising folder for the town. The sticking point proved to be, not suprisingly, money.

"The contention, made by many speakers, that it would prove impossible to raise two hundred dollars for advertising purposes seems to most people to lack foundation, more especially when it is recalled that a booklet costing five times that sum was issued by the citizens of this town a year or two ago," wrote the Tropical Sun reporter covering the story.

".....it seemed the sense of the meeting that if this town could not raise two hundred dollars for advertising expenses it was, indeed, a dead'un."

The Board of Trade's publicity chairman also announced that he had arranged for a full-page ad in the Sunday edition of the Jacksonville Times-Union. In addition, a story in the Christian Science Monitor would provide the city "a little free advertising."

The Board designated October 14, 1913 Board of Trade Postcard Day. A resolution called on citizens to send at least five postcards "to friends in northern states," extolling the virtues of West Palm Beach. People were to be invited to visit or to establish a home "Where Prosperity Beckons."

Tourist clubs were established in West Palm Beach, Lake Worth, Boynton and Delray as well as other smaller towns in the area. Some of these clubs were formed so that people from out-of-state could meet other visitors from their states. After the end of World War I, these clubs formed a special committee to investigate price-gouging of visitors.

In the Roaring Twenties Americans for the first time began exploring their country in a popular new conveyance called an automobile. Dixie Highway offered motorists an avenue into South Florida. They drove in by the thousands, many of them seeing the state for the first time. One result was the birth of the most expansive real estate boom in the nation's history.

A December, 1922 story in the New York Tribune predicted the state would see an unprecedented invasion by 50,000 tourists. The story was headed "Florida — Just Before the Curtain Goes Up." The boom spread the fame of the Palm Beaches across the country. A project for the 1924-1925 winter season asked local residents to mail out 100,000 postcards, bearing "pictures and messages and calculated to draw friends and relatives to the Palm Beaches." The West Palm Beach Chamber of Commerce, better financed than an earlier Board of Trade, published 50,000 publicity booklets, marketing the "best-appearing young men and women" in the area as the "allurements of this section." By 1925 Palm Beach and West Palm

C-8—Whitehall Hotel
Palm Beach, Fla.

Ad campaigns sponsored by Palm Beach and Boca Raton in the 1920s spurred tourism and a real estate boom. This campaign, from 1925, promoted the Palm Beaches as the place "Where Summer Spends the Winter". Photo Historical Society of Palm Beach County

Beach were cooperating in an advertising campaign, utilizing the slogan "Where Summer Spends the Winter."

The boom reached beyond the boundaries of the Palm Beaches. To the north of West Palm Beach a thriving town called Kelsey City was rising on the western shore of Lake Worth. One of its features was the Palm Beach Winter Club, including a clubhouse and golf course. In 1939 Kelsey City became Lake Park.

At the south end of the county the society architect Addison Mizner, whose designs gave Palm Beach its Mediterranean "look," began his program to convert the little farming town of Boca Raton into a world-class resort. With a Hollywood publicist, Harry Reichenbach, as part of his team he launched a major advertising campaign. One series of print ads featured a

g for twelve

fers you a
re it is a joy
neither hot
o July the
ut ten de-

it

unity

yground of
m Beach is
t is a spark-
anent popu-
aining
, and
s even

ends

from the North, a direct cross-state rail-road connection with Central Florida and the West Coast and two main cross-state highways.

A harbor now permits the entry of boats drawing nine feet. By July 1st, 1926 the depth of the inlet will be sixteen feet and the dredging will continue until a depth of twenty-four feet is attained. Aeroplane mail service is now being de-veloped, with a probability of freight service by air in the very near future.

A Back Country of Wonderful Fertility

Back of all there is a firm foundation of agricultural wealth. Palm Beach County offers more than a million acres of the richest land in the world. Much of it is in the heart of the Everglades where Nature has been storing her bounteous resources for untold centuries. No pen can picture the wonders of this garden spot. You simply must come and see for yourself!

colorful description of Boca Raton.

"I am the greatest resort in the world. I have the combined charms of dig-nity, beauty and numerous attractions. I am a place where people of taste can spend a few weeks, a season or the entire year in constant enjoyment. I offer the most even tempered climate in the world. I honestly believe I am the coolest place in the tropics. I can amuse people in many ways. I have as fine a bathing beach as can be found in the tropics. A handsome inn. Beautiful homes. Grand plazas, wide boulevards and streets. Colorful business sections. Theatres showing Broadway plays. Marvelous cabarets. Tennis courts every-where, golf links, a polo field, and a great landing field for airplanes. My future must be glorious."

In Grand Mizner fashion, the graceful cloister, elegant Mediterranean styling and luxurious accents of the Boca Raton Resort & Club have been one of the county's primary tourism assets. Photos Boca Raton Resort & Club.

The boom brought tourists flocking to Palm Beach County. Then in 1926 the "bust" abruptly stopped the flow. Color brochures became black-and-white, ads shrank in size. The demand for new hotels and restaurants dropped as existing properties slid into bankruptcy and by 1929 the rest of the nation had followed Florida into hard times.

In the 1930s the Palm Beaches still offered weather, beaches and accommodations but now the country was broke. The West Palm Beach Fishing Club, founded in 1934, was active in attracting fisherfolk to an area blessed with climate and a variety of ocean and fresh water species.

A new kind of visitor began to arrive after Pearl Harbor plunged America into World War II. Military training camps appeared in the county and such elegant hotels as the Boca Raton Resort and Club became barracks for servicemen.

After the war servicemen and women who had trained here remembered Palm Beach County. They and other Americans whose travel had been restricted by the war began coming to Florida again, both as tourists and as purchasers of winter and year-round homes. Then in the mid-fifties post-war growth received a huge boost as two wealthy and powerful men appeared in the county, one in the south, one in the north.

Arthur Vining Davis, chairman of the Aluminum Company of America (Alcoa), retired to Miami in 1950 and promptly began buying Florida real estate. From the first two letters of each of his names came the corporate title of the corporation he organized in 1958 — Arvida. Davis' company proceeded to develop Boca Raton into the resort Mizner had envisioned — and to promote it heavily on an international scale.

Meanwhile, John D. MacArthur, the second richest man in America, was buying up 100,000 acres of Florida land, much of it in northern Palm Beach County. The sole owner of a major insurance company, he lived in a small suite at his Colonades Hotel on Singer Island. His largest single development was Palm Beach Gardens, to the northwest of Lake Park. In 1964 he persuaded the Professional Golfers Association to move its headquarters to Palm Beach Gardens, where he built a clubhouse and golf courses for the PGA. The arrival of the PGA launched a golfing boom that has given Palm Beach County more golf courses, over 145, than any other county in America.

By the 1980s tourism had grown into a huge industry, involving hotels, resorts, restaurants, attractions, sports and 18 chambers of commerce. In 1981 the county set in motion a plan to utilize bed tax revenues for an expanded and coordinated tourism marketing program. The move created the Tourist Development Council, to provide government oversight, and the Palm Beach County Convention and Visitors Bureau (CVB), a not-for-profit corporation, to market the county's many-faceted tourism delights.

A decade and a half later the move had paid off handsomely for the county. Visitors to the county now run to roughly four million a year,

Facing page: Hot air balloon regatta at PGA National. Thanks to the efforts of wealthy developer John D. MacArthur, Palm Beach County is headquarters for the Professional Golfers Association. With more than 145 courses in the county, more than any other county in America, golf has become a passion for residents as well as a draw for tourists. Photo C. J. Walker.

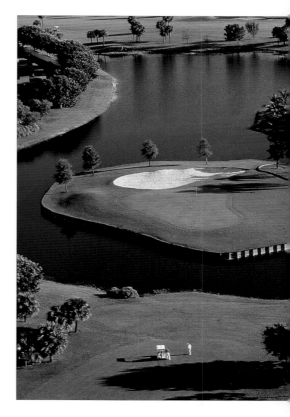

Country Club 18th Hole at the Boca Raton Resort & Club. Photo Boca Raton Resort & Club.

compared to 50,000 predicted for the entire state in 1922.

The reach of Palm Beach County promotions extends not just to the Middle Atlantic and northeast coast and such midwestern cities as Chicago but also to the southwest and to California. CVB offices in Europe, Canada and South America bring in more and more visitors from other lands to enjoy what the bureau calls "The Best of Everything".

A major goal looking ahead to the twenty-first century is to reach out to a new type of tourist, the ecotourist, interested in the outdoors — wilderness areas; scenic rivers like the Loxahatchee, the state's only federaly designated Wild and Scenic River; lakes like the Okeechobee on the western side of the county, and vast agricultural lands in the west. Already in motion are the popular Palm Beach County Growing Tours, which take tourists to such sites as the Callery-Judge Grove and Packing House; the Arthur K. Marshall Loxahatchee Wildlife Refuge, west of Boynton Beach; and the Everglades Reseach Center in Belle Glade.

One hotel served Palm Beach when Flagler arrived a little over a century ago. Now the county boasts more than 200 hotels with over 15,000 guest rooms and more than 2,000 restaurants and night clubs. But perhaps the most impressive measure of tourism's growth is this. In Flagler's day, the season ended on Washington's Birthday. Today it never ends.

Fifty thousand tourists visited the Palm Beaches in 1922. Today, the county offers its exceptional hospitality to approximately four million visitors annually. With 200 hotels offering more than 15,000 rooms and more than 2,000 restaurants and nightclubs there is something for everyone, from families and ecotourists to romantic couples, young and old. Facing page photo Boca Raton Resort & Club. Photo top The Palm Beach Post. Photo left Palm Beach County Convention & Visitors Bureau.

Visitors come from across the U.S., Canada, Europe and South America to enjoy "The Best of Everything" in Palm Beach County. Photo facing page The Breakers. Photos this page Four Seasons Resort.

Palm Beach County offers fresh ocean breezes and fresh Florida taste. Visitors and residents alike indulge in a delightful array of seafood, fresh produce and home grown specialties. The culinary scene has matured in recent years and now boasts eateries from rustic to exquisite and expensive temples of haute cuisine. Photo top C. J. Walker. Photos facing page and left, Four Seasons Resort.

In the Flagler Era, the gracious oceanfront charm of The Breakers hotel in Palm Beach drew the cream of society for the season. Today, the season never ends in Palm Beach County, but the timeless grace of The Breakers remains an international tourist destination. Photo The Breakers.

Lake Okeechobee. Photo The Palm Beach Post/Loren Hosack

Palm Beach
County's
Enterprise

Palm Beach Motor Cars, Ltd.

Along line of famous establishments – Nieman Marcus, Nordstrom, and Saks Fifth Avenue to name a few – have built their businesses on customer service. Palm Beach Motor Cars has firmly placed customer service as their cornerstone – and with spectacular results. From the dream of two salesmen working together on a car lot, to the world's largest Jaguar dealership, this retailer of fine automobiles has gained the respect and admiration of manufacturers, customers and other dealers.

"We've always had very, very strong repeat business," says Palm Beach Motor Cars co-founder Bob Simpson, whose roots in car selling go back to 1945. "We like to put ourselves in the customer's position. What would you want if you came into a car dealership? You'd want to be treated fairly. With respect, with honesty. We know of no other way to do business."

Simpson speaks of a corporate culture which is the result of years of doing business with a handshake; where one's word is one's bond. "I don't know if it's a new idea, or a really old idea, but we've always done business on a relationship basis. We regularly used to extend customers credit for service and parts, because for a customer to have faith in you, you must have faith in them. These little things we did for customers had a cumulative effect over the last 44 years. People talk to each other, you know."

Simpson repeats a story which was told to him by a regular Palm Beach Motor Cars customer. It took place on an estate in Connecticut, where a large dinner party was taking place. After the meal was taken, talk among the men got around to automobiles. It turned out that the majority owned Jaguars. "And, to their amusement, these gentlemen discovered that most of them had purchased their Jaguars at Palm Beach Motor Cars," Simpson finishes, with a chuckle.

Simpson and business partner Norman Gregersen started Palm Beach Motor Cars in 1980 with a total inventory of four used cars and a staff of four. Within ten years, these two entrepreneurs, with a great deal of hard and honest work, had constructed the magnificent 125,000 square-foot facility that is home to Palm Beach Motor Cars today.

Left to right: Robert Simpson Jr, executive vice.president; Robert Simpson Sr, president; Mark Simpson, vice president.

Palm Beach Motor Cars continues the tradition of providing luxury automobiles to Palm Beach County residents that began over 60 years ago in the old Packard dealership on South Dixie Highway in West Palm Beach. Army Air Corps veteran Simpson joined his father in the automobile business in West Palm Beach in 1946. From 1952 to 1979 Simpson marketed Rolls Royces and other first-class foreign automobiles in South Florida.

Meanwhile, food industry consultant Norman Gregersen and his wife, Sonia, owned and operated a classic Rolls Royce business in Ft. Lauderdale, Florida from 1973 until 1979. That same year the Simpsons and the Gregersens formed a partnership to acquire Palm Beach Motor Cars. The West Palm Beach dealership is now located on the corner of

The world class showroom of Palm Beach Motor Cars.

Left to right: Sonia Gregerson, operations manager; Collette Restly, comptroller; Richard Langley, office manager.

Okeechobee Boulevard and Dixie Highway, where customers can browse a fantastic selection of Jaguars, Aston-Martins, Land Rovers and Lotus automobiles, plus a huge collection of certified pre-owned cars from makes like Jaguar, Mercedes Benz, Rolls Royce, Bentley, Saab, Porsche and more.

By 1996 Palm Beach Motor Cars had become the world's largest retail Jaguar dealer, world's largest retailer of Jaguar convertibles, and sellers of the most used Jaguars per capita in any single market area. But customer service did not get left behind with increasing sales: the dealership also ranks among top Jaguar dealerships in customer satisfaction.

"Early on we recognized the trend of customers to expect a lot more service from dealerships than they were getting," says Palm Beach Motor Cars General Sales Manager Ed Sheppard. Sheppard's office is walled completely with glass between his desk and the main showroom floor, mainly so people can see that he is there and available. "We responded by offering pick-up service for repairs and maintenance, especially in outly-

ing areas. This seemed to start a trend of other area dealers offering more service for their customers. But, we've always tried to keep at least two steps ahead."

Sheppard explains that customer satisfaction begins and ends with listening to, and hearing, the customer. "In a world a main topic of conversation at cocktail parties or while playing golf is cars, it's especially important to give customers a very satisfying experience, so that they speak favorably about you and your product. That's why we've devoted so much time, money and energy to making sure our customers are happy.

"If someone does have a problem we do whatever it takes to satisfy the customer, but we go a step further and attempt to compensate the customer for their time and inconvenience. This is where other organizations sometimes fall short of the mark," says Sheppard. Palm Beach Motor Cars will arrange car rental, detail the car, or make some other meaningful gesture in order to "make it right." In Sheppard's words, "Being right doesn't keep a customer. It's important to recognize and accept responsibility for any perceived problem, and to find an individual solution in each case."

Sonia Gregersen, wife of co-founder Norman Gregersen, acts as Palm Beach Motor Cars' top customer service officer, making sure that customers are treated right, and that Palm Beach Motor Cars retains their standing as an active, involved member of the civic community.

Gregersen says satisfying cus-

Left to right: Jim Jackintelle, used car manager; Mark Simpson, vice president; Ed Sheperd, general sales manager.

Left to right: sales consultants; Glynn Evans, Les Melvin, Jay Vogele, receptionist Jennifer Anthony, sales consultants, Don Cody, Rich Mathews, Terry Jahrsdoerfor.

tomers is easy. "All you have to do is be honest," she says, "and the rest all falls into place." Gregersen believes in telling the truth 100% of the time, not just when it's convenient, or when it suits one's own needs. "If you make a mistake and we all do, you know, we're human – you say so, not only with our customers, but with each other here at the dealership. We respect each other, and are loyal to each other. All of the satisfied customers and sales records come from this attitude."

"This attitude" – even in the service department – of taking care of the customer first translates to all areas of the dealership. From the receptionist in the showroom to the sales staff and management, at Palm Beach Motor Cars there is the customer – and no one else.

Most of all, Palm Beach Motor Cars is known for their selfless involvement in the community of West Palm Beach. Through the founding partners and their families, Palm Beach Motor Cars has helped to raise millions of dollars for worthy children's causes within the city. Sonia Gregersen, wife of co-founder Norman Gregersen, was instrumental in the development of Connor's Nursery, Florida's first facility for children with AIDS and HIV. More

often than not, the parents of children with this incurable disease are too sick to care for their own children. Connor's Nursery, opened in 1990, was the answer to this heartbreaking situation.

"A lot of people say, 'I can only give a little bit, so I might as well not even bother.' This keeps a lot of people from participating. What they don't realize is that if each of us gives just a little, the aggregate is enormous.

It makes a huge difference. When I started, I too felt that I didn't have enough time or money to really make a difference. But once you get started, you get hooked. It's more than just a philanthropic philosophy, it quickly becomes a way of life."

Palm Beach Motor Cars has also supported The Children's Place, a 24-hour-a-day facility for abused and neglected children, opened in 1979. And through their work with the Association for Retarded Citizens, Palm Beach Motor Cars supports various children's services including infant development, pre-school education and training, day care for at-risk infants, and five housing facilities.

What is the secret of keeping some of the world's toughest customers some of the world's most happy customers? Treat them better than you would expect to be treated yourself. For instance, let's say you have need to bring in your car for regular service. First imagine what it's like when you go to the typical car dealership repair shop. Now, let yourself imagine that you are driving into the Palm Beach Motor Cars brick-paved covered verandah and reception area. When you approach the service area, you will be greeted by highly trained Palm Beach Motor Cars "Service Advisors."

Left to right: Service advisors, Bob Bohm, Bill Sheehan, Hank Miller, Joy Baroni, Mike Magyarosi.

"We cater to every whim of our customers," says Service Manager Jim Baroni, "We genuinely want to make customers happy. This isn't just a job for our Service Advisors, we really enjoy what we do – and customers pick up on that."

Baroni says that his Service Advisors develop a relationship with each customer, and each service appointment is followed up with a phone call to make sure everything's just right. Baroni says that people come to rely on Palm Beach Motor Cars to the extent that they call when they're looking for cars for their kids and they want to have them checked out, or if they're having problems with one of their other cars. "We're like one big, extended happy family," says Baroni.

A Service Advisor is the customer's primary contact with a Palm Beach Motor Cars service department. These experienced experts are not paid a commission on what the customer spends. They are paid a salary, so there is no pressure to sell any service or repairs that may not be necessary. In fact, the only "bonus" received by these Palm Beach Motor Cars team members is based solely on customer satisfaction ratings, as indicated by one of the numerous satisfaction surveys conducted by Jaguar Car, Inc. In this way, the service team is completely focused on the customer's needs, instead of their own.

The head of the service depart-

Jim Baroni, service manager.

ment is available to all customers at all times. At any time, if any customer feels they have a problem that is not being addressed or wishes to lodge some sort of complaint or concern, there is always a company principal or officer present to speak with them directly. Because of the family-based

Sam Samuel, parts manager.

structure of the company, the owners and partners of Palm Beach Motor Cars extend an "open door" policy to all of their customers.

If a customer's car is going to stay in Palm Beach Motor Cars' service area more than briefly, the company will arrange for alternate transportation, usually in the form of a rental vehicle. Further, all service customers, whether receiving an oil change or having a transmission replaced, gets their car washed free of charge.

When a customer returns to pick up their car, they deal directly with the same Service Advisor who greeted

them, not a cashier. Typically at other dealerships, cashiers are the people who returning customers must deal with. At Palm Beach Motor Cars, Service Advisors make sure that customers completely understand all charges, and answer any question about the invoice directly.

How did Palm Beach Motor Cars manage to make it to the top? A lot of personal devotion, a lot of heart, and a lot of customer satisfaction. And in return, they get a lot of their own satisfaction knowing that they've made West Palm Beach an even more beautiful place to live.

The team at Palm Beach Motor Cars believes in building long-term relationships with customers, and strives to keep them year after year. In fact, the staff members, many of whom have worked there since the early years, feel that they are part of an extended Palm Beach Motor Cars family. It is this dedicated group of hardworking individuals that maintain Palm Beach Motor Cars' "Customer First" philosophy; taking great pride in selling some of the world's finest automobiles with the utmost in honesty, integrity and professionalism.

Jim Jackintelle, used car manager.

Jesse Newman & Associates

It would be harder to find a single aspect of life in Palm Beach that Jesse Newman has not influenced, than it would be to name all those he has:

Business, banking, the arts, education, tourism, law enforcement, civic life, philanthropy, health. It's little wonder that they call him "Mr Palm Beach". And it's no wonder at all that the phone rings constantly at the offices of Jesse Newman & Associates, a consulting firm specializing in public relations, community relations and business development.

Long before the formation of the firm, however, Jesse Newman was a key player on the Palm Beach business scene as well as a public relations powerhouse. Whether attending a social gala or presiding over a Chamber of Commerce meeting, he could be heard touting the attractions of Palm Beach with passion.

Newman had his bar mitzvah money in his pocket, a World War II stint in the navy behind him and plans for a vacation in Miami when he stopped in Palm Beach to visit friends in 1951. He never left.

In those days, private railroad cars and mule-drawn trolleys still spotted the lush avenues of Palm Beach, while Mrs. Margery Merriweather Post reigned over the social scene from the glittering halls of Mar-a-Lago. Jesse Newman saw it all — from the palm trees to the potential — with the eyes of a young optimist fresh from New York.

In addition to his suitcase, Newman brought a degree in economics and business administration from St. John's University, the beginnings of a law degree and a strong family background in the retail business with him to Palm Beach. He made his mind up to stay and opened The Lullaby Shop, a children's retail clothing store located on Palm Beach's illustrious Worth Avenue.

Within four months of his arrival, Newman met his future wife, Helene. Working together, the couple established themselves in the heart of Palm Beach's most exclusive shopping district and in the lives of many of the town's families. "After ten years in business," Newman says, "we realized we were going to lose some of our kids because they were outgrowing the children's wear featured at Lullaby." Instead of saying good bye to their young clientele, Newman opened The Prep Shop.

The Newmans are credited with convincing the designers at Lacoste to produce a children's line of their classic alligator shirts. And word has it that they were the ones who introduced area residents to what would become the quintessential Palm Beach fabric — madras.

But it was the business that introduced Newman to a galaxy of dignitaries and stars. The signatures of John F. Kennedy, Robert Kennedy, Perry Como, Truman Capote, Judy Garland, Elizabeth Taylor and Barbara Walters featured in a framed collection of canceled checks elicit fond memories for Newman.

"It was easy for Ethel Kennedy to call me on the phone and order 20 pairs of chinos," he recalls, "She had five boys — she needed that many!" The Kennedy children grew up, but scores of new families from Hobe Sound to Boca Raton flocked to Newman's doors on Worth Avenue, for school uniforms.

As the years flew by on the gentle ocean breezes that caress Palm Beach, Newman continued to seek out challenges and opportunities. From 1957 to 1969 he was President of the Worth Avenue Association. He has served on the Board of Directors of at least 17 organizations, including the Palm Beach Civic Association, Palm Beach Crime Watch, the Palm Beach County Convention and Visitors Bureau, the Palm Beach County School of the Arts Foundation, Trustee of Flagler Museum, Trustee Palm Beach Community Chest and Community College Foundation. He is Chairman of The Palm Beach Code Enforcement Board and has served on the Zoning Landmarks Preservation and Architectural Commissions. He is also the recipient of the Guardian of the Menorah Award from the Lt. Col. Netanyahu Unit of B'nai B'rith, and Vice Chairman of The Palm Beach Fellowship of Christians and Jews.

After a quarter of a century of memories and achievement, he sold his retail operations and ventured into banking, serving as a founding director and senior vice president of The Worth Avenue National Bank for six years.

Newman's enthusiasm next took him to the eastern end of Worth Avenue, where he contributed his energy to the formation of the Esplanade, overseeing the distinctive shopping complex from its ground breaking until it was fully leased in 1983. At that point, it seemed only natural to open the doors of Jesse Newman & Associates, specializing in public relations, business development and community relations.

Since 1971, Newman has held the office of President of the Palm Beach Chamber of Commerce. It is a role ideally suited to his experience and his personality. "We're concerned with preserving the high level of business and professional ethics that have earned Palm Beach its cachet," he explains, "The caliber of our residents and our world-class shoppers deserves to be met with an equally high caliber of service from business owners and employees."

As President of the Chamber of Commerce — or in any one of his many roles — Jesse Newman speaks with passion, evidence that the love affair with Palm Beach that began for him more than 45 years ago has not dimmed.

Newman is perpetually young. He zips around town, around home, around the world like a man one-third his age.

Judge Knott Center For Historic Preservation

In the 1960s and 1970s increased urbanization and the loss of historic sites led to the formation of several private organizations and public agencies to restore historic buildings and preserve the disappearing heritage of Palm Beach County.

In 1960 Whitehall reopened as the Henry Morrison Flagler Museum in Palm Beach. The Historical Society of Palm Beach County, organized in 1937 and revived by Circuit Court Judge James R. Knott in the late 1950s, was invited to move its collection into the new Museum.

Efforts by other like-minded citizens in the county led to the formation of the Palm Beach County Genealogical Society (1964), the Delray Beach Historical Society (1965), the Boynton Beach Historical Society (1968), the Boca Raton Historical Society (1972), the Loxahatchee Historical Society (1972) in Jupiter, the Glades Historical Society (1976), the Preservation Foundation of Palm Beach (1980), the Museum of the City of Lake Worth (1982), Old School Square (1986) in Delray Beach, the Boynton Women's Club Historic Preservation Foundation (1986), and Yesteryear Village (1990) at the South Florida Fair in West Palm Beach.

Public sector initiatives to preserve our local heritage led to the establishment of historic preservation ordinances and programs in Boca Raton (1975), Palm Beach (1979), Delray Beach (1987), West Palm Beach (1990), Palm Beach County (1993), and Lake Worth (1996).

The Boca Raton Historical Society was instrumental in the creation of the Historic Boca Raton Preservation Board by the Florida legislature in 1974 and the new state agency was invited to locate with the society in the historic Town Hall. In 1975 Judge Knott swore in the first Board of Trustees appointed by the governor. In the early years, the society and the preservation board conducted a survey of historic properties, established a local preservation ordinance, and listed several properties in Boca Raton on the National Register of Historic Places.

Recognizing the need for these successful programs throughout the growing county, the Florida legislature renamed the Boca agency the Historic Palm Beach County Preservation Board in 1984. John P. Johnson was appointed director of the agency in 1985 and expanded HPBCPB programs to other parts of the county. The HPBCPB established

Circuit Court Judge James R. Knott. Photo courtesy of Mort Kaye Studios.

The Judge Knott Center for Historic Preservation was dedicated in 1995 by Secretary of State Sandra Mortham. The Center is located in the Old School Square Historic District in Delray Beach.

awareness of heritage activities, conducted historic surveys in other communities, sponsored the Mizner Symposium (1987-1990), nominated significant properties to the National Register of Historic Places, and coordinated the installation of state markers at historic sites. The agency conducted the first survey of historic resources in the unincorporated areas and drafted the historic preservation element of the Local Comprehensive Plan for the county. The agency also published the first heritage tourism brochure to encourage visitation to historic sites open to the public throughout the county. The HPBCPB provided a local liaison for historic preservation grants, publications, and services available from its parent agency, the Florida Division of Historical Resources in Tallahassee. Historic Palm Beach County was incorporated as a private not-for-profit direct support organization in 1989 to assist the HBPCPH in fund raising activities.

In 1993 the Historic Palm Beach County Preservation Board entered into a joint venture with the City of Delray Beach and the Community Redevelopment Agency to rescue two houses from demolition in West Palm Beach and relocate them via barge to downtown Delray Beach. The project to create two public agency offices was

named the Delray Beach Historic Houses Infill Project. During the relocation and rehabilitation phase of the project in the Old School Square historic district, the HPBCPB temporarily moved its office to the Cason Cottage Museum, a restored property of the Delray Beach Historical Society.

Secretary of State Sandra Mortham dedicated the Judge James R. Knott Center for Historic Preservation on October 28, 1995. The Monterey-style house, designed in 1939 by the Palm Beach master architect Belford W. Shoumate, was named to honor Judge Knott for his long and distinguished service to historic preservation and local history. Over the years he served as president and president emeritus of the Historical Society of Palm Beach County, president of the Preservation Foundation of Palm Beach, and chairman of the Palm Beach County Historical Commission. Judge Knott's love of history led him to write a series of articles known as the "Brown Wrappers" in the Sunday *Palm Beach Post* and in retirement he published a three volume series on Palm Beach County history.

The Judge Knott Center offers programs that increase awareness about the value of preserving our cul-

tural resources for future generations. The center features a preservation library, seminars in historic preservation, and a gallery for exhibits of architecture, art, and Florida history. The center directs its effort toward educating the public about the benefits of preservation and provides consulting services for local preservation initiatives. These services include targeting cultural resources, assisting local government to meet comprehensive planning requirements, and identifying sources of funding. These efforts encourage development of the local economy through increased tourism and additional tax revenues. The center seeks recognition for significant local sites and historic districts while maintaining affiliations with state and national historic preservation organizations.

In 1997 the Delray Beach Historic Houses Infill Project received a *Meritorious Achievement Award for a Non-Residential Rehabilitation* from the Florida Trust for Historic Preservation. In a major reorganization of state preservation efforts, the 1997 Florida legislature did away with the Historic Palm Beach County Preservation Board. Today, the Judge Knott Center has become a Regional Office of the Florida Division of Historical Resources.

The Social Science Building by night.

Florida Atlantic University
'The miracle on Glades Road' comes of age

Thirty-three years ago, President Lyndon Johnson squinted in the bright October sun as he gazed across an abandoned World War Two airfield in the sleepy community of Boca Raton and declared Florida Atlantic University officially open. In actuality, FAU — the fifth public university to be established in Florida and the first one south of Tampa — had welcomed its charter class of 867 students the month before. They arrived on September 14, 1964, to a campus with almost no trees, just a few buildings, parking lots crisscrossed by fading landing stripes, and a flagpole bent like a pipe cleaner by the fierce winds of Hurricane Cleo.

The campus may have lacked a collegiate atmosphere, but from the very beginning both students and fac-

ulty members imbued the new state university with a strong sense of academic purpose. The first students were all commuters, and many were beyond traditional college age. They pursued their degrees with businesslike seriousness, quickly establishing a fine reputation for the young educational institution. Indeed, the transformation of an oil-stained South Florida airfield into a regional center of intellectual activity took place so rapidly that the university's founding president, Dr. Kenneth R. Williams, exaggerated only slightly when he described FAU as "the miracle on Glades Road."

Today, FAU's six rapidly growing campuses dot the coastline of Florida. Under the vigorous leadership of its fourth president, Dr. Anthony James Catanese, FAU has

Dr. Anthony James Catanese, President and Professor, Florida Atlantic University.

become the fastest growing university in Florida and possibly the entire

FAU students enjoy a study break outside the Education Building.

country, with campuses in Boca Raton, Davie, Fort Lauderdale (both downtown and on Commercial Boulevard), Palm Beach Gardens and Port St. Lucie.

The quality of education offered is so high and the tuition costs so low that FAU has been named one of the "100 best college buys in the U.S." by an independent consumer magazine. Fully accredited by the Southern Association of Colleges and Schools, FAU also regularly scores high marks in U.S. News & World Report's national college and university rankings.

Academic programs include 54 terminating in bachelor's degrees, 45 in master's degrees, and 14 in doctorates. Among the university's areas of excellence are ocean engineering, brain science, computer science, elementary education, the arts and humanities, accounting, nursing, and public administration. In 1996-97, almost 20,000 degree-seeking students were in attendance.

Through its Division of Continuing Education and Open University, FAU provides working

and retired adults a broad selection of career advancement and personal enrichment classes at convenient locations in Broward, Palm Beach and St. Lucie counties. And FAU's Lifelong Learning Society, the most successful program of its kind in the country, delivers stimulating classroom experiences to an ever-growing number of senior learners — 15,000 at last count.

Thanks to the generosity of the late philanthropist Charles E. Schmidt, FAU boasts one of the best endowed colleges of arts and humanities in the country. The $10 million Dorothy F. Schmidt Center for Arts & Humanities was dedicated in 1994 by Governor Lawton Chiles. The record-setting Schmidt gift also provided funding for two Eminent Scholar chairs which, when filled, will add two more world-class scholars to FAU's distinguished faculty. Eminent Scholars already in residence include internationally respected authorities in the fields of brain science, high-definition television, engineering, nursing, community education, Holocaust studies, theatre, philosophy, and sociology.

Six of the university's eight colleges are based on the Boca Raton campus. They are the Schmidt College of Arts & Humanities and the Colleges of Business, Education, Engineering, Nursing, and Science. Residence halls and a modern apartment complex provide housing for more than 1,500 students.

In Palm Beach Gardens, FAU classes are being conducted temporarily in leased space at NorthCorp Center, just east of 1-95 off PGA Boulevard, pending a move in 1999 to a 135-acre campus in Jupiter's Abacoa planned community. The Jupiter campus will include a broad selection of upper-division and graduate degree programs and the first four-year Honors College in the U.S. to be built from the foundation up. The mission of the Honors College is to provide a top-flight liberal arts educational experience to a select group of academically gifted students.

FAU's Port St. Lucie campus offers an ever-expanding number of complete undergraduate and graduate degree programs to students living on the Treasure Coast.

Two of the university's colleges are based on its Broward County campuses: the College of Liberal Arts is headquartered in Davie and the College of Urban & Public Affairs is housed in the Reubin O'D. Askew Tower in downtown Fort Lauderdale. Dozens of complete degree programs are available on the Broward campuses, including recently introduced degree programs in architecture and physical therapy.

With the approach of the 21st century, FAU is emerging as a prototype of the new urban region university, with full-service campuses distributed across a large service area and a demand-oriented approach to higher education. With more than 3,500 employees on its payroll, the university generates an astounding $1.1 billion in economic activity annually. "The miracle on Glades Road" has proved to be a blessing not just for Boca Raton and Palm Beach County, but for all of Southeast Florida.

Fran Murphy Interiors, Inc.

Step into the Fran Murphy building and you step into an upscale mini design center, the culmination of a business journey that began more than 30 years ago.

investment group, Fran purchased a 165,000 square foot building and named it the D & D Center of the Palm Beaches. Her 45,000 square foot showroom, filled with luxurious furniture, accessories, and outstanding art and sculpture, was recognized as the "most outstanding, exciting, designer showroom in the country".

In August of 1985, Fran introduced her own line of electronic furniture for national distribution. The collection featured electronically oper-

"Ribbon Dancer," in Turkish Onyx. One of many works of fine art displayed in the Fran Murphy Showroom.

Fran literally grew up in the furniture and accessory business. She was setting vignettes in her family furniture store when she was ten. Her desire to go beyond the furniture store led her to Florida State University and to the University of Miami, where she studied Design. Following her educational experiences, Fran went to work for a design firm in Miami's Designers Row.

Anxious to apply her individual

The Fran Murphy Building in Juno Beach on U.S. Highway One. Three floors and 50,000 square feet of design center merchandise. One stop shopping for your entire home.

creativity to design projects, and with the grand sum of $900 in the bank, Fran opened her first designer showroom in Miami. What followed was a number of individual and commercial assignments, including the Jockey Club in Miami.

Through referrals her business increased and Fran found herself drawn more and more to luxury residences and commercial projects in Palm Beach County. So, following the axiom of being where the business is, Fran opened her first Palm Beach designer showroom in a 15,000 square foot facility at the corner of Clematis Street and Railroad Avenue, in West Palm Beach.

In 1981, as part of a real estate

ated built-in component wall units custom designed for individual needs.

While the introduction, of the electronic line focused attention on Fran's furniture design ability, the fact is that much of the furniture shown in her showroom is designed by Fran. At private showings, manufacturers frequently ask for Fran's input as to what she feels would enhance the look and acceptance of particular items of furniture.

Wanting to bring together a more complimentary and cohesive

Accessories are everywhere in the Fran Murphy Showroom. From traditional to contemporary, attractively displayed as room vignettes.

Fran Murphy, established Fran Murphy Interiors more than 30 years ago. She and her staff make clients' home dreams come true.

group of luxury designer showrooms that would be available to the public as well as the design trade, Fran purchased a building in Juno Beach, about ten miles north of Palm Beach.

This was a major move for two important reasons. One, Fran would have the responsibility of selecting tenants that by complimenting each other would provide a one stop shopping experience, and two; all the showrooms would be open to the public as opposed to designers only.

Today, the Fran Murphy Building is home to the finest in luxury furnishings, accessories, kitchens, baths, closets, window, floor and wall treatments, a luxury home builder and architect, and the latest in home elec-

Ten foot console is a coral top, cut and finished by Tim Murphy to fit an antique base.

Fran Murphy, established Fran Murphy Interiors more than 30 years ago. She and her staff make clients' home dreams come true.

tronics and home theatre. Fran's third floor showroom features an outstanding selection of furniture, traditional as well as contemporary, displayed in art gallery settings with dramatic lighting. The furniture, much of which is custom designed, is complemented by the latest in electronics and a collection of contemporary and antique art and sculpture.

Fran's staff consists of ASID designers, a professional architect, and resources that include a fabric and wallpaper library. She has an 18,000 square foot warehouse facility with a large inventory of furniture and decorator items for immediate delivery.

Fran Murphy's three children all work in various aspects of the design industry. Carol Murphy, a graduate

Fantasy Bed. An original design of Fran's executed by a local metal artist and finished in gold leaf.

designer, has a portfolio of commercial and luxury residences that is second to none. Michael, the architect, has engaged in some commercial design but is most proud of the multi-million dollar residences he has designed in the Palm Beach area, as well as in other parts of the country. Tim Murphy studied with an internationally known artist and has developed into a recognized artist in his own right, working in marble and stone. A number of his sculptures are displayed in the Fran Murphy Showroom.

In order to truly appreciate what people in the trade call the "most outstanding showroom", you have to experience it for yourself.

The Weitz Company, Inc... And the Building of Palm Beach County

Charles Weitz emigrated to America in 1850 with the idea of using his skills as a builder and carpenter to carve a name for himself in a young, growing country. Little did he know that nearly a century and a half later, the Weitz name would continue to be carved on a variety of building projects across the nation.

From its modest beginnings in Des Moines, Iowa, in 1855 The Weitz Company, Inc. has grown into a nationally-ranked, full-service general contractor and construction manager with a solid presence in many of the country's major metropolitan areas including Denver, Omaha, Phoenix, and West Palm Beach.

Since 1978, Weitz led the way in the construction and renovation of some of South Florida's most recognizable landmarks. Building on a heritage of craftsmanship and service, Weitz has become one of the most respected and trusted names in the construction industry today — in the country, the state, and in Palm Beach County.

The company's first building projects in Florida were retirement villages, such as The Waterford in Juno Beach. Since then, Weitz has built 19 retirement communities and assisted living facilities throughout South

Florida, providing area residents with 3,094 senior apartments, 746 beds, 108 assisted living units, and 50 units for the care of Alzheimer's patients.

The Weitz Company then diversified its efforts to contribute in numerous ways to other areas of the community. Weitz built libraries for the enrichment of the county's residents and projects such as Meyer's Amphitheater Bandshell beautify the downtown district and provide a focal point for the community. The

Benjamin School of Fine Arts, Florida Culinary Institute, Palm Beach Atlantic College, and William T. Dwyer High School represent Palm Beach County's varied educational opportunities and The Weitz Company's range of construction expertise.

Weitz is an integral part of the County's retail background also, having built shopping districts such as Plaza Del Mar, Shoppes of Boynton, Congress Square, and Wedgewood Commons. At The Breakers Retail Specialty Shops, built by Weitz, a unique shopping experience awaits residents as well as non-residents of the area.

Palm Beach County is well known for its hospitality and its hotels. The Weitz Company has been proud to contribute to the area's reputation as a world-class destination, from the restoration of gracious historic landmarks to the construction of luxurious contemporary hotels. Once the playground of this country's early industrialists, the century-old Breakers Hotel remains the crown jewel of Palm Beach. Through a long standing relationship, Weitz continues to oversee renovations in the older parts of

Above: The Waterford, one of the first retirement communities built by the Florida Division of The Weitz Company, includes apartments, a health center, and a commons area.

Left: A glass curtain wall system reflects a typical Floridian sky at the Flagler Office Building in downtown West Palm Beach.

Through each successive generation, the Weitz family stood behind each and every project with a commitment to customer service, superior performance and reliability. Total quality management, in both the service provided and the final product, has always been the cornerstone of The Weitz Company's efforts.

The Weitz Company continues to be recognized and presented with awards for excellence. Weitz was honored nationally for the construction of the Kravis Center for the Performing Arts Parking Ramp in West Palm Beach. The project's schedule, design, and cost objectives were all met and most importantly to the community, parking was readily accessible when the Center opened for the next season.

Quality construction, however, isn't the only way The Weitz Company strengthens the community. The firm is an active member of the West Palm Beach Chamber of Commerce, Palms West Chamber of Commerce, The Chairman's Club, Economic Council, Executives' Association of the Palm Beaches and the Business Development Board of Palm Beach County. The firm also promotes and contributes to local charity fund-raising events, as it continues to stay committed to its role as an integral member of the community.

Charles Weitz may not have been able to predict the future in 1855, but he would be proud to know that the ideals upon which his company was founded have remained constant today.

the hotel as well as assisting in transforming new visions into reality. For modern tropical luxury, guests can enjoy the Ritz-Carlton in Manalapan, another example of Weitz quality in construction.

The Weitz Company has also been involved in many of the more practical aspects of life in Palm Beach County, from transportation to processing and manufacturing, including the Palm Tran Satellite Facility in Delray Beach, the Sundown Manufacturing center in Boca Raton (national headquarters for Rexall), Palm Beach Bedding (Serta) in West Palm Beach, and several United Parcel Service (UPS) projects.

Whether Weitz is building a manufacturing plant or enhancing a cultural landmark, each project the company undertakes embodies the commitment of four generations of the Weitz tradition. A philosophy embracing honesty, integrity, craftsmanship and pride are Charles Weitz's legacy — and the driving force behind the company's continuing success.

Today, that legacy underlies all company policies, such as the Design-Build cooperative efforts between The Weitz Company and the architects which yield a more efficient, proactive approach to construction. Combining architectural and engineering services produces significant advantages and a strong foundation for all Weitz projects. The team approach adhered to by Weitz means everyone is involved and informed, from the client to the crane operator, and provides a meaningful forum for the exchange of ideas.

The Weitz Company takes pride in keeping pace with the latest technological advancements. Managers in the office can oversee field operations through computerized and standardized software solutions that are sophisticated and yet functional for day-to-day routines. Weitz is also accessible on the Internet (http://www.weitz.com), utilizes a sophisticated Extranet for project control, and maintains an Intranet for information sharing.

Above: While the Breakers Hotel remained in operation as usual, The Weitz Company renovated over 500 rooms in this century-old structure.

Left: Mediterranean architecture, stained glass windows, and interior courtyards separate Palm Beach Atlantic College from its plainer sisters.

Lynn University

Lynn University is a private, coeducational institution offering master's, bachelor's and associate degrees. The University was founded as Marymount College, a two-year school for women.

Beginning operation in 1962, Marymount became a candidate for membership in the Southern Association of Colleges and Schools in 1964 and was accredited in 1967 at the earliest possible time.

During the 1960s, the College flourished. Buildings were built, programs set in motion and enrollment increased with each new year. As the College entered the 70s, its fortunes changed. Declining enrollments and budget deficits forced the Board of Trustees to announce in September 1971 that the College would close in May 1972.

Donald E. Ross, then President of Wilmington College, visited the campus in the fall of 1971 to purchase library books from Marymount College. He immediately saw a challenge and a promise in the failing school. In December 1971, largely due to the efforts of President Ross, Marymount and Wilmington Colleges formed a consortium structured for

Lynn University's serene campus is the perfect setting for living and learning in south Florida.

Dr. Donald E. Ross, president, Lynn University.

the benefit of both institutions. It was a unique affiliation that saved and revitalized the failing school.

The early 1970s was a tumultuous period for the College. President Ross assumed responsibility for an institution deeply in debt and under-enrolled. He acted decisively and instituted major organizational changes. Efforts were directed at expanding career concentrations such as hospitality, business administration, art, pre-elementary education

and fashion while retaining a solid core of general studies requirements unifying all programs. The focus was on quality education and on doing a few things well rather than diluting energy through proliferation of objectives. In 1974, the institution was renamed the College of Boca Raton.

The College fully recognized its need to increase community involvement on the campus and to make a name for itself in the local and regional areas. Drawing the community into the campus was accomplished through the creation of advisory boards in various disciplines. At the same time, the College entered the work world through extensive practica carefully integrated into the career programs.

With two-year programs strengthened and consolidated under a revised core curriculum, its finances

The new $6.2 million Lynn Library with state-of-the-art technology is the heart of the academic enterprise at Lynn University.

stabilized and with community acceptance and recognition, the College was ready to move forward once again. In taking the step toward accreditation as a Level II institution, the College recognized it was taking somewhat of a risk, as it did in 1971 when the odds were against the failing, private College. But a few believed in a revitalized College of Boca Raton and it was those few, through dedication and sacrifice, who created a thriving institution.

In December 1986, the College was accredited by the Southern Association of Colleges and Schools to offer four-year degree programs. Today, bachelor's degrees are offered in over 30 concentrations, the newest of which are pre-med and environmental studies. In 1988, the College received accreditation for master's degrees and offers the Master of Business Administration, Master of Science and Master of Education. In 1998, the first doctoral program will be initiated. As the College entered the last decade of the 20th century and looked at the type of institution it wanted to be in the 21st century, a number of priorities emerged:

- to continue to develop viable career oriented programs that respond directly to the challenges of the times
- to build strong upper division arts and sciences curricula that will provide the core for all of the institution's majors and programs

- to develop "institutes" or "centers of excellence" that will attract national leadership and provide the environment for creative thinking and research
- to construct, establish and/or renovate campus facilities, resources and programs that will enhance student life and augment the academic enterprise.

Adhering to these priorities, the Board of Trustees followed the institution's goal of national and international expansion by making the decision to attain university status and in September 1991, the College was renamed Lynn University.

Since President Ross took the reins, four buildings have been built and several of the original buildings were completely renovated. The recently completed Lynn Library is a state-of-the art facility housing over 90,000 library material units including books, microforms, videos and other audio/visual formats. Completed in 1992, the 35,000 square feet de Hoernle Sports and Cultural Center includes a gymnasium, locker rooms, meeting rooms, a conference center and offices. In the newest residence hall, the Lynn Residence Center, rooms have private baths and there is

a fitness center on the first floor. Occupancy is limited to students carrying 60 credits or more. The Schmidt College Center was opened in 1984 and houses administrative offices. The de Hoernle International Center will begin operation in the fall 1997. The facility combines classrooms, administrative and activities areas for the rapidly growing international population, a large multipurpose meeting room, reception area and 250 seat auditorium.

In 1993, American College Dublin was founded. Lynn University's sister campus in Ireland offers bachelor's degrees in a variety of disciplines as well as a study abroad program for college students and high school students. The College was accredited by the Irish higher education accrediting agency in 1996 and graduated its first class that same year. Part of the Ireland campus is the boyhood home of Oscar Wilde and the College recently acquired facilities that will provide housing for students. The International Student Residence Hall is just a block away from the campus and three blocks from Dublin's City Centre.

Worldwide affiliations have been developed in Japan, France and Argentina. The University has a partnership with Katoh Schools and Fuji Phoenix College in Gotemba, Japan. As part of the educational experience students live with Japanese families and Japanese students stay with host families when they attend Lynn.

Future plans call for further expansion of the campus to include residences, classrooms and office facilities. New programs are under consideration and as demand requires, bachelor's, master's and doctoral programs will be introduced. Lynn University believes that today's students need to have an international perspective to prepare them to succeed in today's increasingly global economy. Based upon that belief the University will continue to seek opportunities in the international spectrum to provide the best possible education for its students.

Town Center at Boca Raton

Spaning 123 acres in the heart of Boca Raton, the attractions of Town Center appeal to local residents all along Florida's southeastern shores as well as to visitors from even farther afield.

Boca Raton, the southernmost city in Palm Beach County, is one of the bright lights on South Florida's Gold Coast. Bordered by the Atlantic Ocean to the east and the Everglades to the west, it is little surprise that Boca Raton is a major tourist destination. Apparently though, not even the area's great wealth of natural attractions can rival one other significant local destination. Since Town Center at Boca Raton opened its doors in 1980, visitors routinely cite shopping as their number one pleasure activity.

From a comfortable perch on a charming replica of a New York City Central Park bench surrounded by green trees and lush plants reaching toward majestic skylights, shoppers can anticipate the pleasures to be found in Bloomingdale's, Burdines, Lord & Taylor, Saks Fifth Avenue, Sears and 150 upscale specialty shops, and restaurants.

Perhaps their adventure will begin by encountering prominent names such as Polo Ralph Lauren, Joan & David or Louis Vuitton and conclude with a friendly visit to familiar favorites like Banana Republic, Ann Taylor and Brookstone.

The Market Place beckons browsers to a colorful arcade of shops adorned with old world signs. After following the inviting promenade through the Market Place archway, a view of The Grove unfolds. The aroma of fresh coffee and baked goods, spicy snacks and the many other specialties conveniently served by a cluster of 17 quick service restaurants provides a temptation.

There are still so many shops to explore, but now the idea of a cool drink and some light refreshment combines with the welcoming atmosphere presented by The Grove's skylit seating and tropical landscaping is an invitation to dally.

Hand-glazed Mexican tiles in rich shades of cobalt and terra cotta draw the eye and the shopper on to the Fashion Court. Still more rewarding discoveries await in The Burdines Court. Water happily cascades down the sides of a pyramid into a bubbling modern fountain while squares of living trees soar upwards to the skylights.

While irresistible shopping and entertainment opportunities brings tourists, international travelers and area residents together, Town Center's innovative architecture brings the old world together with the new. Inside at the Great Center Court, bubbling fountains, lush trees and picturesque seating areas capture the essence of the great public spaces of Europe. Trailing plants, hanging from a gallery level catwalk above adorn the Great Center Court with a lush, green crown.

Sixty-five benches, a 25-foot post clock and cast stone fountains were custom designed and hand fabricated by the internationally renowned Kenneth Lynch & Sons of Connecticut to faithfully recreate the stately charm of original designs produced more than a hundred years ago. Lynch himself, an octogenarian designer of decorative metal objects, a blacksmith and the only fabricator of suits of armor in this country, is a wise and genial Irishman who adds the luster of his own history to that of the great traditions evoked by his creative custom reproductions. Among his more notable assignments have been the wrought iron gates enclosing the baptismal in St. Patrick's Cathedral in New York, a 25-ton altar canopy for a seminary chapel and a suit of armor for a daft, but wealthy gentleman who fancied himself as William the Conqueror.

Much of the inspiration for the Center's design, however, remains home grown. Echoing the vision and skill with which famed Florida architect Addison Mizner shaped the distinctive character of Palm Beach County's historic architecture, Town Center's interior evokes the quintessential flavor of Boca Raton's gracious traditions. In contrast, the exterior presents an eye-catching blend of modernistic glass and pyramidal skylights accented with triangular entryways, soothing off-white stucco, hand-glazed tiles, sloping tile roofs in warm earthy tones and tropical landscaping.

"Much of the character and design of the Center was derived from trips to Europe and Vizcaya Gardens as well as from the Mizner architecture," says architect Thomas Witt of RTKL, who spent six months studying Boca Raton before turning to the drawing board. "We tried to make it a very pleasant place," he says in a true understatement.

Town Center's elegant ambiance is nothing less than appropriate for Boca Raton, one of the most affluent market areas in the country and one of the fastest growing business centers in South Florida. The shopping mecca is not only appropriately designed, but is also appropriately named. Town Center is located near the epicenter of the city, just east of Interstate 95, South Florida's major north-South thoroughfare. Midway between Boca Raton's traditional eastern hub and the rapidly growing western suburbs, Town Center truly is at the center of activity. Since opening, it has functioned unofficially as the primary shopping destination in Boca Raton.

Brown Distributing Company, Inc.

Brown Distributing Company is an independent distributor of quality Anheuser-Busch products, including Budweiser, Michelob, and Busch beer. The company has been in business since 1936, was incorporated in 1951 by father and son, Abraham and Jacob Brown, and operates in West Palm Beach, Florida and Richmond, Virginia.

The business origins of Brown Distributing Company date back to 1919, when Abraham Brown started a soft drink bottling company. The Budwine Bottling Company featured a cherry-cola flavored carbonated beverage called "Budwine." In 1926, Abraham acquired the franchise for Try-Me Beverage, a line of flavored drinks. Business flourished over the next few years, and following the repeal of prohibition, Abraham entered into the wholesale beer business, distributing a Philadelphia brewed beer called Wolf Beer.

In January, 1935 Try-Me Bottling Company received an exclusive franchise from the fledgling Pepsi-Cola Company to manufacture and distribute Pepsi-Cola, and in February, 1936, Try-Me was also appointed by Anheuser-Busch, Inc. as the exclusive distributor for its beer products, namely Budweiser. Due to the growing popularity of Budweiser, Abraham and Jacob Brown were inspired to form Brown Distributing Company as a separate company for beer distribution only.

In 1973, Larry Brown entered into the business, representing the third generation of the Brown family. He was elected president in 1983, and in 1984 headed the acquisition and development of a new Brown Distributing Company located in West Palm Beach, FL. Under Larry's leadership, the West Palm Beach location has grown from an operation of 65 employees to one employing over 145 people. Dedicated to providing quality service and products, Brown Distributing Company hires a broad cross section of individuals, representing the diverse cultures of South Florida. In 1988, Larry's wife, Betty, was brought on as Vice President and Director of Consumer Awareness and Education. For its commitment to excellence in community involvement, Brown Distributing Company and its principals have won several awards, including: The prestigious Ambassador Award, presented by Anheuser-Busch, in recognition of maintained standards of excellence in business; the 1996 Outstanding Philanthropic Organization Award, given by the Palm Beach County Chapter of the National Executives; and the 1997 Excellence in Enterprise Award, which recognizes outstanding business leaders of Palm Beach County.

A History of Community Involvement
Brown Distributing Company has a long-standing commitment to the community. Serving as President and Vice President, respectively, Larry and his wife, Betty, understand the importance of philanthropy, service, and giving back to the community. They share a special interest in the youth of our community, and believe that youth

Top: Providing quality Anheuser-Busch products since 1984, the West Palm Beach branch of Brown Distributing Company is a prominent business in the community. Photo by Barry Kinsella.

Left: Serving as President and Vice President, respectively, of Brown Distributing Company, Larry and Betty Brown are very active in community events and philanthropic efforts.

Two students learn computer skills and participate in a wide variety of other fun and educational activities at The Little Brown School House.

are our most valuable resource. Together, and through the auspices of Brown Distributing Company, they have founded, supported, and championed many worthy causes and are actively involved in a variety of local community volunteer projects and events. The Browns have established, through their company, scholarship funds at four different colleges, and helped to establish a student scholarship fund through the CAREing Foundation, a not-for-profit organization which they founded in 1995 to produce and fund youth-oriented, educational arts programs which focus on drug and alcohol abuse prevention. Larry and Betty Brown also founded The Little Brown Schoolhouse, a day care facility owned and funded by Brown Distributing Company and operated by a professional staff.

The Little Brown School House

Offering reasonably priced, quality, convenient child care services for children of employees and the general public since 1991, The Little Brown Schoolhouse has served as a model for other businesses to learn how to implement this important employee benefit. Under the guidance of Larry and Betty Brown, a governing Parent's Advisory Board, and the daycare staff, new and effective educational programs have been developed and implemented to stimulate the children's motor skills and creativity.

Consumer Awareness Programs

Brown Distributing Company has taken a leadership role in consumer education and actively supports programs that educate youth to help pre-

vent underage drinking. The company offers to its customers and to the community several consumer education and awareness programs (CE&A) to prevent drunk driving and illegal consumption by minors. One of the CE&A programs is the "TIPS" (Training for Intervention Procedures by Servers of Alcohol) training classes, which teaches servers how to recognize signs of intoxication in customers, check for valid IDs, and to intervene effectively with potential drunk-driving situations. These classes are given in Brown's community meeting facility, use of which is provided free of charge to local organizations.

The CAREing Foundation, Inc.

The CAREing Foundation is a collaborative community partnership, dedicated to providing opportunities and resources for young people to develope their own innovattive, artistic approaches to reach their peers with messages about the dangers of substance abuse. Its mission is to produce and fund on-going, youth-oriented, educational arts programs that carry anti substance abuse messages and that use a peer-to-peer approach to prevention.

Larry and Betty Brown have effectively worked with arts and prevention education since the early 1980's and feel that kids could be just as receptive to positive peer pressure as they are to negative peer pressure. With the help of community leaders, other organizations, and CAREing Foundation members, The CAREing Foundation formed the CAREing Partnership, which sponsored a *KIDS TO KIDS™* Prevention Program and

also commissioned a musical to be written by kids for kids. The musical that was written, entitled *We-The Living,* is comprised of a series of real-life short stories that depict the difficulties faced by young people who are confronted with alcohol, drugs, and negative peer pressure. It was written, scored, and performed by the students at the School of the Arts, with input from students at the South Area High School, and premiered at the Raymond F. Kravis Center for the Performing Arts in West Palm Beach, FL, in March of 1996. In 1996, more than 12,000 students saw live performances of *We-The Living.*

Since that time, the *KIDS TO KIDS™* Prevention Program has evolved into a multi-faceted educational arts program that involves youth and volunteers from across the county. President and founder, Betty Brown, says: "For us, the key to making effective change is working with leaders in the community who want to join together to make a positive difference in the lives of our young people." *KIDS TO KIDS* is designed to involve students in the arts, while building their self esteem and resistance to negative peer pressure. In addition, the program is designed to provide role model opportunities for students by placing them in key leadership positions. The ultimate goal of the program is to reduce the number of youth who participate in substance abuse.

Brown Distributing Company encourages community involvement and volunteerism in its employees by setting a good example. The Browns also encourage and challenge other companies, who are not already active in their communities, to explore the many different ways that they can support their communities and their community leaders.

As part of the business leadership of Palm Beach County, Brown Distributing Company is committed to providing quality service and products, maintaining a diverse workplace, and supporting the community of Palm Beach County. The company looks forward to continued growth and success into the next millennium.

The Chesterfield Hotel... A sparkling jewel in the heart of Palm Beach

A rose by any other name would smell as sweet. The words are Shakespeare's, but the sentiment is particularly appropriate when applied to The Chesterfield Hotel. Since opening in 1926, this lovely Palm Beach hotel has had many suitors, many name changes and a few face lifts. Throughout its long and charming history, however, The Chesterfield Hotel has remained a sweet bloom in the heart of Palm Beach.

The hotel first shone on the Palm Beach stage in 1926 under the billing of the Lido-Venice. Its Mediterranean-style architecture was complimented by a Venetian decor and its opening was heralded by local press and dignitaries alike. In 1928, the name was changed; for more than 50 years this gracious star would be known as Vineta.

In 1990, after being purchased by its current owner, renamed, rejuvenated and awarded the Mobil four-star and AAA four diamond ranking, the four-story hotel was designated an historical landmark.

Shakespeare's sentiments could never have been more appropriately applied to The Chesterfield than now. Elegant surroundings, antiques, fresh flowers and a welcoming glass of sherry envelop guests in a gracious English country-manor ambiance.

While Shakespeare may have preferred a rose, The Chesterfield blooms with red carnations. The signature flower is worn by staff members ready to familiarize guests with the comforts of the 55-room hotel, from the warmth of a wood-paneled library with its inviting fireplace to the country house charms of accommodations decorated with antiques, designer fabrics and marble bathrooms.

Traditional English tea is served in the afternoons... with freshly baked scones and delectable clotted cream.

From intimate shadows the ghosts of past guests, celebrities and owners mingle with those who currently grace the elegant hallways. The spirit of John L. Volk, the prolific Palm Beach architect who oversaw the hotel's renovations in 1937, must surely approve of the luminaries from the international world of fashion, theater, politics and society who have fallen under The Chesterfield's spell.

Oscar de la Renta favors the Library. Eartha Kitt believed the stunning decor of the renowned Leopard Lounge and Supperclub, which recaptures the glamour and exuberance of the 1940's cabaret era, was created

A stay at the Chesterfield is unlike any other, enveloping you with unparalleled service and uncommon elegance. The superb location, just off Worth Avenue in the heart of Palm Beach, makes this charming four star hotel perfect for business or pleasure. Stroll to the shores of the Atlantic or the famous shops on Worth Avenue.

exclusively for her. Former Prime Minister Margaret Thatcher developed a partiality for the sun-deck attached to her fourth floor penthouse suite during the first of her three highly-secured visits to the hotel. George Hamilton is a regular in Churchills, the premier cigar room, providing elegant surroundings which offer the perfect setting for guests to relax with the distinctive taste of a pleasurable "puff," while enjoying a fine cognac or vintage port.

With each new guest that enters its historic environs, The Chesterfield Hotel unfurls its beauty anew. And, with Worth Avenue, the sparkling shores of the Atlantic Ocean and the unmistakable panache of Palm Beach all within reach, the bloom is sure to stay on this rose.

Ta-boo

Left to right: Nancy Foote Sharigan, owner; Don Scherzi, pianist; Franklyn P. deMarco, Jr., owner.

For more than 50 years, the speciality of the house at Ta-boo, an American Bistro and Bar on the island of Palm Beach, has been éclat.

Since opening its doors on Worth Avenue in 1941, Ta-boo has catered to such notable patrons as the Duke and Duchess of Windsor, Frank Sinatra, Peter Lawford, the Kennedy clan, Gary Cooper and Richard Nixon. If you listen to the insiders, you'll hear how Betty Hutton, suffering from a headache, ordered the first Bloody Mary from a sympathetic bartender at Ta-boo. Or you may hear the legend of the German U-Boat officers who, during World War II, secretly came ashore to enjoy the nightlife at Ta-boo before returning to the tedious business of sinking American ships.

The Hollywood crowd frequented Ta-boo from its earliest days, when Gable, Gabor, Dietrich, Flynn and Stewart held court. Today, you may see Don Johnson, Jessica Lange, Oprah Winfrey, Bobby Short, Rod Stewart, Michael Caine, Lou Rawls or Stephanie Powers enjoying the bewitching ambiance of Ta-boo's British West Indies decor.

Under the direction of Nancy Foote Sharigan and Franklyn P. deMarco, Jr., Ta-boo serves more than the discriminating palettes. The restaurant plays an active role in the community, sponsoring charity and civic activities.

Ranked alongside Harry's American Bar in Paris and "21" in Manhattan as one of the world's top bars, Ta-boo offers courteous, informed service, sensible prices and a range of exciting menu items that continue to make it a favorite spot to see and be seen.

Lunch and dinner specialties, such as tender veal chops, Maine lobster, Dover Sole and crisp main course salads, are available in any of the restaurants five distinctive dining areas. Enjoy Roasted Black Duck with an Orange Blossom Honey Ginger Sauce from a table by the fireplace or a lusty pesto, calamata olive and mozzarella pizza appetizer from a romantic spot in the Courtyard Room. Choose from an extensive — and intriguing — wine list while you share a private moment with someone special in the Gazebo Room.

Relax with soothing music in the Bistro Room. A piano keeps Ta-boo in tune with the times, past and present — when the weekend dancing isn't in full swing, that is. The front Terrace lounge, with its original 1940s lattice work and the feel of a sidewalk cafe, is ideal for people watching.

At Ta-boo, every table is graced with a delicate rose and every seat is wrapped in the mystique that has made this such a special place in Palm Beach history.

This cozy fireside dining room is just one of five spacious rooms – graced with rich fabrics, Victorian patterns and Mediterranean accents.

Gulden Real Estate

Palm Beach County is the largest county in the U.S. east of the Mississippi. "You can drive all the way across the state of Maryland in less time than it takes to drive from one end of Palm Beach County to the other," says Dorothy Engels-Gulden. She should know. Since coming to Palm Beach in 1966, she has made it her business to know. Literally.

To be more precise, Gulden, better known to friends, clients and several generations of the county's leading families as "Rusty," has translated her knowledge of the county and its diverse real estate into $350 million dollars worth of business.

The traditional aspects of life in Florida, epitomized by the town of Palm Beach, appealed to Gulden from the beginning. The area's heritage of refined coastal living and dynamic native growth, combined with Gulden's appreciation of them, became the building blocks of success.

While working for Palm Beach architect Eugene Lawrence, Gulden obtained her Florida real estate license. In 1971, she joined the Palm Beach Board of Realtors. In 1977, she represented the Southern Realty Group in the purchase of Martin Downs, a 2,400-acre residential and commercial subdivision in Stuart. From 1977 to 1979, she managed the $45 million sellout of Sun and Surf, a luxurious six-acre property on the Atlantic Ocean in Palm Beach.

In 1979, Gulden opened her own real estate office on Sunrise Avenue in Palm Beach and in 1986, she took the helm as vice-president for the company-owner of Leverett House (on the ocean on Sunset Avenue), a 21-unit, private, luxurious, award-winning apartment building.

In addition to gaining a reputation for brokering the sale of private island mansion residences and luxury condominiums, the firm specializes in handling commercial-zoned land for influential development projects including hotels, shopping centers and office buildings as well as the purchase

and sale of established commercial investment properties. Gulden understands the economy and trends and has various personal investments (real estate, of course) along the Gold Coast as well as a retirement home in Devon, England. She has renovated, constructed and developed properties for her own account during her long career.

Gulden's full-service, personalized approach to business reflects her understanding of the unique needs of Palm Beach residents and investors. The office is small, private and very professional; a boutique of real estate needs. To enhance the service she pro-

Top: Gulden Real Estate has a reputation for brokering the sale of private island residences.

Left: Dorothy "Rusty" Gulden.

vides to this respected clientele, Gulden earned a license from the National Association of Securities Dealers in 1983.

Gulden's extra efforts on behalf of her clientele were quickly rewarded, both in terms of personal satisfaction and professional achievement. Recently, Gulden closed sophisticated deals involving approximately $20 million and 110,000 square feet of prestigious office space represented by L'Pavilion in North Palm Beach and The Horizons in West Palm Beach.

In addition to being a member of the Palm Beach Board of Realtors, Gulden is also a member of the Palm Beach Chamber of Commerce, the Florida Association of Realtors, National Association of Realtors and the National Association of Real Estate Appraisers. She has served on the advisory board of a Palm Beach branch of a major bank. She is also a corporate member of the Palm Beach Civic Association and serves on many community-oriented committees and boards.

Fairbanks Communications, Inc.

The air in Palm Beach County is freshened by sea breezes and blue skies. Waves tickle the shore. Palm Beach County has a look all its own. And a sound all its own.

In addition to the air and the waves, the air waves are an integral part of the region's character. From the hit songs on a radio keeping sunbathers company on the beach, to the vital news broadcasts keeping a diverse population informed and the reliable weather and traffic reports keeping people and their businesses moving, radio reaches people across the county, in their homes, cars and offices as well as in the South Florida sunshine.

Fairbanks Communications, Inc. has made a commitment to the com-

Top left: The old building where the WRMF and WJNO studios were located for decades, until 1996. Although they are now in temporary facilities, all four of Fairbanks Communications, West Palm Beach radio stations are moving into its own brand-new building by the end of 1997.

munity, to serve its radio broadcasting needs, and as an active corporate member of the Community, to participate in the rich life of Palm Beach County and its residents.

Formed in 1948 by Richard M. Fairbanks, Fairbanks Communications has owned radio stations in Indianapolis, Dallas, Philadelphia, Kansas City and Boston. Since 1983, the company has made West Palm Beach its corporate headquarters and has actively begun centralizing all of its radio operations in South Florida.

Fairbanks Communications takes pride in being "South Florida's Home Town Team." In Palm Beach County alone, Fairbanks listeners can tune in to the soothing sounds of WRLX-FM 92. 1; news, talk and sports on *WJNO*-AM 1040; country music and the comments of Howard Stern on WCLB-FM 95.5; the contemporary music mix of WRMF-FM 97.9, whose call letters derive from the initials of the company's founder; or WJNA-AM Unforgettable 1230, broadcasting with an overwhelmingly popular nostalgia format.

Up the road a bit, WIRA-AM 1400 also broadcasts a nostalgia format, and WJNO's northern sister station for local news, weather, traffic and sports WJNX-AM 1330, both serve the Treasure Coast.

Unlike many radio broadcasting companies which have adopted a revolving door approach to ownership in the shifting South Florida market, Fairbanks Communications continually invests both human and financial capital in the community. A member of the Florida and Palm Beach Chambers of Commerce and the Palm Beach County Business Development Board, the company envisions a long-term future in the area.

Fairbanks Communications' commitment to the future includes an investment in the area's children. In 1985 the firm established the Fairbanks' Children's Fund. Fairbanks Communications absorbs the entire cost of operating the Fund so that all money raised can be distributed among 70 agencies serving underprivileged children in the region.

The future of Fairbanks Communications envisions sounds good for Palm Beach County.

Boca Raton Community Hospital

"A tradition of excellence with the personal touch."

Boca Raton Community Hospital, 800 Meadows Road, Boca Raton, Florida.

to the hospital. In October 1982, Boca Raton Community Hospital reached its planned capacity of 394-beds.

Today the largest hospital in southern Palm Beach County, Boca Raton Community Hospital offers many specialized services, some of which include: the nationally recognized Lynn Regional Cancer Center; the Women's Center and Center for Breast Care; One Family Place maternity and pediatrics; SurgiCenter Plus and Pain Management Service; a Rapid Care Center; The Therapy Center; Outpatient Nutrition Center; and Home Health Service. The hospital offers a full array of educational and support programs, free screenings and outreach programs including those provided through a special partnership with Boca Raton Fire-Rescue Services called Smart Heart. The School Nurse Program, the first of its

Boca Raton Community Hospital was the first known hospital in the nation to provide a registered nurse to each of its city's (17) public elementary, middle and high schools as a free community service.

Caring for its community for over three decades, Boca Raton Community Hospital has a rich and compassionate history. It was the tragic deaths of two children, Debbie and Randy Drummond, in 1962 which became the impetus for building a hospital in Boca Raton. At that time, Boca Raton was a city of 10,000 people with the nearest hospital 20 to 30 minutes away. The Debbie-Rand Foundation was organized by influential residents who shared the common goal of building an institution to serve the healthcare needs of this rapidly expanding city in southern Palm Beach County. The Debbie-Rand Memorial Service League was chartered in September of that year by civic minded women to raise funds and coordinate volunteer services toward the establishment of a hospital as proposed by the foundation.

By July 1964 the foundation had nearly completed a drive for one million dollars in public support. The present sight of the hospital, 25.6 acres on Meadows Road, just south of the

Florida Atlantic University campus, was selected and approved by the city commission in January 1965. Ground was broken in November 1965, and the foundation changed its corporate name to Boca Raton Community Hospital.

The four story, 104-bed hospital opened its doors on July 17, 1967. In 1968 the board announced a $7-million expansion program, and by 1971 six floors were added, bringing the total number of beds to 250. At that time the sixth through eighth floors were "shelled in" for later expansion. By 1977, these remaining floors were completed, and growth of the coronary medical and surgical intensive care units increased the total inpatient capacity to 344 beds. This $17.5-million expansion program added many new services including a radiation oncology department which would later be named the Lynn Regional Cancer Center and be complemented with a satellite facility in Delray Beach. In addition, a state-of-the-art education center, with its modern 251-seat auditorium, was opened adjacent

kind in the country, has been providing a registered nurse in each of Boca Raton's 17 public elementary, middle and high schools as a free community service since 1994.

The hospital is fully accredited by the Joint Commission on the accreditation of Healthcare Organizations and its cancer program is designated as an approved program by the American College of Surgeons.

Royal Palm Travel

Susan Lehrman-Blank, the founding owner of Royal Palm Travel.

The distinctive charm of Palm Beach has evolved not only from a bounty of natural beauty but from the wealth of ideas, style and experiences residents bring to the area from around the world. Susan Lehrman-Blank adds to that charm.

As the founding owner of Royal Palm Travel, she has dedicated her personal and professional skills to the specialized travel needs of Palm Beach's unique clientele. Since 1977, she has nurtured the successful growth of a business while designing custom travel itineraries that range from sea kayaking adventures with whales in Alaska to luxurious retreats in the private villas of Europe.

Royal Palm Travel specializes in foreign independent travel. Lehrman-Blank and a full-time staff of 16 travel specialists possess an in-depth expertise that extends from Europe to the Baltic States, Orient and South Pacific. They have developed long-standing professional relationships that facilitate arrangements with foreign and domestic airlines, cruise ship companies, railroads, hotels – both here and abroad – and tour companies, when appropriate, as well as yacht and air plane charters.

In addition to researching travel journals and schedules, Royal Palm Travel agents enhance their education and expertise by exploring exceptional domestic and international locations. Their personal experience of the various cruise ships and airlines allow them to make reliable, up-to-date recommendations, to the agency's sophisticated clientele.

This valuable repository of first-hand knowledge allows Royal Palm Travel to provide such special services as world-wide restaurant recommendations and reservations, theater tickets, shopping advice and personalized scenic itineraries for driving tours whether self-driven or chauffeured.

Not surprisingly, Royal Palm Travel's agents are also knowledgeable in obtaining the required documentation such as visas when booking their clients independent travel.

Royal Palm Travel is a member of API, an association of premier agencies pooling their resources to provide the discriminating traveler with unique value-added amenities. Royal Palm Travel also participates in API's Navigator program, offering soft adventure and special interest trips for the more sophisticated traveler seeking a singular journey.

The agency uses a state-of-the-art computerized airline system to advise clients immediately of the most current and economical fares available. While serving the commercial and domestic travel needs of many clients, approximately 90 percent of the agency's business remains dedicated to international leisure travel. Through Lehrman-Blank's involvement with the boards of many local charities, hotels and cruise lines, Royal Palm Travel also aids in arranging member-sponsored benefit cruises for such organizations as Adam Walsh Children's Fund, Dana Farber Cancer Institute, Salvation Army, Rotary International and Intracoastal Health Foundation. It is all part of her contribution to the charm of the community.

The Palm Beach Post

For more than 80 years, The Palm Beach Post has served Palm Beach County as the area's primary newspaper. Read each day by more than one-half million people, The Post also serves as a valuable business partner to start-up and established businesses alike. And with a new flagship building, designed by West Palm Beach architectural firm Gee & Jenson and completed in 1995, The Palm Beach Post is poised to lead Palm Beach County readers into the information age of the 21st century.

The Palm Beach Post has its origins in the earliest periodicals established in Palm Beach County as a weekly newspaper called the Palm Beach County in 1908. In 1916, the name was changed to The Palm Beach Post, and it became a daily newspaper. A Palm Beach businessman,

Edward Bradley, bought both The Post and an afternoon paper, The Palm Beach Times, in 1934. In 1947, John Holliday Perry Sr. bought both papers and in 1948, purchased the Palm Beach Daily News as well as Palm Beach Life magazine.

These four publications came of age in 1969, when the highly respected Cox Enterprises of Atlanta, Georgia, bought Perry's group and renamed the company Palm Beach Newspapers, Inc.

Still more changes lay ahead. In 1979, the afternoon paper was renamed The Evening Times and in 1987 merged with The Post to form one dynamic daily morning newspaper called The Palm Beach Post. Palm Beach Newspapers also publishes the Palm Beach Daily News and the Florida Pennysaver, a weekly shopper.

From locations on Clematis and later Datura Streets, the newspaper moved into its current location at 2751 South Dixie Highway in West Palm Beach. The Post maintains six community news bureaus, as well as reporters and news bureaus in Tallahassee and Washington, D.C., and has 13 distribution centers throughout its circulation area and the state.

In the past several years, as the county steadily moved toward its one million population milestone, The Post's circulation also increased. Average year-round circulation nears 175,000 copies each day and 225,000 copies on Sunday. The Post is in the top 100 newspapers in the U.S. ranked by circulation.

As Palm Beach County's primary newspaper, The Palm Beach Post's editorial staff of 240 talented individuals is diligent about keeping readers informed about their community. The Post's reporters, editors and photographers consistently win national, regional and state awards for outstanding photography, news coverage, features, design and editorial writing. As part of Cox Newspapers' worldwide news network, The Post has access to the finest national and international reporting as well.

The Palm Beach Post also shares in the responsibility to serve the community, helping to improve the quality of life for the county's residents. The Post makes ongoing contributions and serves as sponsors to literacy and education, the arts, human service organizations, and to helping feed the hungry. Every year, The Post recognizes and rewards outstanding law officers in Palm Beach, Martin and St. Lucie counties, and awards scholarships to local graduating seniors.

With a deeply rooted history in Palm Beach County, award-winning journalism, and the most technologically advanced facility, The Palm Beach Post is committed to providing readers the most thoughtful, in-depth coverage. From around the world ... and around the block.

"Each morning, more than 500,000 residents in Palm Beach County and the Treasure Coast wake up to the award-winning Palm Beach Post."

PGA National

PGA National: this 2,340-acre resort community is world-renowned for its successful combination of real estate, commerce and recreational facilities.

It was over an idle lunch conversation in 1976 that E. Llwyd Ecclestone and the then Director of the PGA of America discussed the growth of Palm Beach County and PGA of America's need for a corporate home in South Florida. At that moment the concept for PGA National took shape.

Today the 2,340-acre resort community is world-renowned for its successful combination of residential real estate, commerce and recreational facilities.

Development began on PGA National in 1979 in Palm Beach

Gardens. It now contributes a large job base to surrounding municipalities and provides nearly 5,000 homes. It also serves as a venue for major national and international sports events.

PGA National features five 18-hole tournament golf courses, a world-class spa, a fitness center, 19 clay tennis courts, and five tournament-size croquet lawns. It is also home to the Professional Golfers' Association of America, the largest organized sports association of its kind.

The AAA Four Diamond and

Top: E. Llwyd Ecclestone, chairman of National Investment Corporation and general and managing partner of PGA National.

Left: The best of both worlds come together at PGA National with golf, real estate, resort, recreation and commerce facilities.

Mobil Four-Star PGA National Resort & Spa features 339 guest rooms, 80 cottages and 7 restaurants and lounges. The hotel's award winning conference center is recognized as one of America's premiere conference destinations and offers 30,500 square feet of meeting space.

The Spa, opened in 1992, is unique and has added a wonderful lifestyle amenity to the community. It features the "Relaxing Waters of the World" mineral pools and offers some of the world's most advanced programs and services, from massage, skin care, nutrition, and fitness training to gourmet spa cuisine.

The Golf Club at PGA National includes the nationally acclaimed Academy of Golf at PGA National, five golf courses, seven putting greens, three driving ranges and a well-stocked pro shop. Adjacent is a Private Member's Club.

Attention has been focused on PGA National many times as it has played host to prestigious golf tournaments including the International Ryder Cup Matches and the PGA Championship. In April 1998 it will host the PGA Seniors' Championship for the 16th time.

In addition to hosting players of all skill levels and age ranges, the PGA National Health & Racquet Club has been the site of some outstanding tennis matches. Club facilities include state-of-the-industry workout equipment, aerobic and dance studios, personal fitness training, racquetball, a lap pool, and snack bar.

Currently under construction is a 338-unit life care community which will include a clubhouse and health-care facility. Rounding out the commercial facilities are a shopping center, office park and commerce park.

Llwyd Ecclestone was considered a visionary when he started PGA National. This landmark community continues to set the pace for quality living and has become an international mecca for sports, fitness, dining and entertainment.

Port of Palm Beach

The Port of Palm Beach is Florida's fourth busiest container port.

Palm Beach County's coastline offers more than miles of sandy beaches and balmy ocean breezes for the delight of residents and visitors alike. Coastal access to the busy international shipping lanes of the Atlantic and Caribbean through the Port of Palm Beach has created a gateway to the Americas and added an integral element to the County's economic base.

The Port of Palm Beach District, established as an independent special taxing district by the state in 1915, is now Florida's fourth busiest container port. Nationally, in rankings by the American Association of Port Authorities, the Port of Palm Beach is the 21st largest in container throughput with total annual cargo tonnage approaching four million short tons.

Historically, the Port has acted as a magnet, attracting private sector marine related industries. By taking advantage of technological advancements and port infrastructure, the Port continues to promote growth and maintain its active role in the county.

By developing modem capacities related to current trends in containerized shipping, the Port provides a dynamic link to domestic rail and road distribution systems. It is the only port facility in South Florida operating its own rail system. With eight miles of rail tracks, pier-side rail box, hopper and intermodal cars operate 24 hours a day keeping pace with a thriving international trade. The Florida East Coast Railway Company (FEC) offers service to the docks and piers through the Port's industrial rail switching operations. Additional rail service is provided through CSXT at off-dock Port Properties.

Every year bulk sugar, molasses, cement, utility bunkers, water and various grades of aggregate materials, among other cargoes, flow through the Port of Palm Beach. In addition to its intermodal capacity and role as a major trans-shipment point for such goods, a combination of Foreign Trade and domestic Enterprise Zones increase the Port's attractions, contributing to the flow of another valuable commodity — jobs.

Also flowing through the Port — at an expanding rate of more than 300,000 annually — are cruise line passengers. Operated under The International Maritime Organization's security standards, the Port's cruise terminal offers air-conditioned comfort and jetway convenience for travelers.

In its proactive mission to serve the regional community, the Port's Board of Commissioners, elected at large by voters within the District, collectively promote the advantages of conducting international trade through the Port's 5,600 linear feet of piers and 200-plus acres of waterfront property. With their unique perspective on the attractions of Palm Beach County's coastline, the Port's commissioners and executive staff have plotted a course for the future that involves a number of enhancements to the Port's ability to serve cruise and cargo vessels as well as the community.

Hardrives, Inc.

George Elmore did more than discover the road to success in Palm Beach County — he paved it.

t all began in 1953 when Elmore founded Hardrives, Inc. He started off with a commitment to client satisfaction, a strong belief in the value of honesty, loyalty and personal attention in business; and a $125 contract to pave a driveway. Today, Elmore oversees a multi-million dollar company with a name that is synonymous with road work and paving throughout the region.

From the firm's distinctive headquarters in Delray Beach, Elmore has guided the company's growth with a common sense approach, a sensitivity to the area's natural environment and an open door policy. The results speak for themselves.

Hardrives still handles contracts for driveway construction and paving, but the company has grown right along with the county, taking on ever more challenging projects. As traffic and population pressures in the area increased, Hardrives was involved with sections of Interstate-95 and numerous projects on both major and arterial roadways including State Road 710 and U.S. Highway 1. When student enrollment and curriculum expanded at Florida Atlantic University, Hardrives was responsible for access roads, new parking areas and a range of courts at the athletic complex.

Elmore has built not only a solid reputation but a solid team, one that is capable of all the work involved in constructing, platting and paving driveways, parking lots, highways and major residential and commercial developments.

From the paving of the first driveway to the construction of Interstate-95, Hardrives has provided each client with the Personal attention and technical expertise needed to complete each project in a timely, cost-effective manner.

The firm is justly proud of its

Top: Delray Asphalt Plant — This is a CMI Triple Drum Plant. It is a State-of-the-Art facility with air emissions of less than 15% of permitted standards.

Left: Road Widening Project — Widening sections of Military Trail from two lanes to six lanes.

clients, including the Florida Department of Transportation, the Florida Board of Regents, Palm Beach Community College, the School Board of Palm Beach County, Palm Beach County Engineering Department and the Arvida Corporation. The firm is under contract with dozens of municipalities and nearly every major developer in Palm Beach County.

What Elmore feels says more about the company than anything else is that these and other clients

return, year after year, to entrust Elmore and his team with new and more demanding undertakings.

From the clearing and grubbing of South Florida's often inhospitable land, through excavation, site grading, laying of pipe and base preparation, to asphalt work, sealcoating, signage and striping, Hardrives has been intricately involved in shaping the area's growth for more than 40 years and is, even now, busy laying the foundation for Palm Beach County's future.

Florida Crystals

Florida Crystals grew from a small farm founded in 1960 by the Fanjul family, when they became political refugees after Fidel Castro seized power in Cuba. Alfonso Fanjul, Sr. and his family began again by purchasing 4,000 acres of land in western Palm Beach County and acquiring three defunct Louisiana sugar mills, which they reassembled to form the Osceola sugar mill.

Today, Florida Crystals is a fully-integrated producer of natural sugar and rice products. The company farms more than 180,000 acres, operates three sugar mills, two sugar refineries, a rice mill and two renewable energy power plants in western Palm Beach County. Florida Crystals markets a variety of natural cane sugar and rice products to natural foods stores across the United States and the Caribbean. Florida Crystals produced the first certified organic rice in Florida and introduced the first certified organic sugar ever produced in the United States. We are a leader in developing and implementing the concepts of sustainable agriculture, including crop rotation, wildlife resource management, biological pest control, and renewable energy power production. Our farms support a diverse base of wildlife native to the Florida Everglades, including deer, alligators, and many species of endangered wading birds.

Through the New Hope Foundation, Florida Crystals is able to help thousands of less fortunate people in western Palm Beach County communities. The New Hope Foundation sponsors the Redlands Christian Migrant Association Family Center in Pahokee, which serves over 130 disadvantaged children by providing food, day care and education. The Association also has a Youth Center, which provides educational, recreational and health programs to 65 youths 10 to 17 years in age. A new health care facility at the Family Center provides free or low-cost medical care for local people in need. The health care facility is a cooperative

effort with St. Mary's Hospital and Everglades Regional Hospital, and includes an obstetrics and pediatric care unit.

Top: Our Sem-Chi (short for Seminole Chief) rice mill produces a variety of rice products, including white, brown, jasmine and basmati.

Lower Left: Florida Crystals' farms support a wide variety of endangered wading birds, such as wood storks, herons, egrets, and roseate spoonbills.

Lower Right: The Florida Crystals and Sem-Chi brand lines include a full line of natural, minimally-processed sugar and rice products.

JFK Medical Center

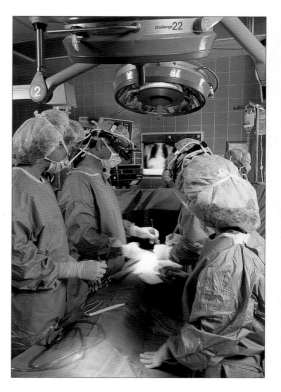

JFK Medical Center, a 363-bed acute care hospital, outpatient center, and medical office complex on a 23-acre campus in central Palm Beach County, offers an extensive array of services and cutting-edge specialty programs in a warm, caring and patient-focused environment. The facility is a recognized leader in open-heart surgery, oncology, orthopedics, neuroscience and women's health services. The Heart Institute at JFK Medical Center is nationally acclaimed for its advanced cardiac services and excellent patient outcomes.

The medical center opened in February, 1966 as Lake Worth General Hospital with a 150-bed capacity. In 1967, the facility's name was changed to JFK Medical Center. Through the years, JFK has become a respected regional medical center, attracting patients from throughout South Florida and the Treasure Coast. The JFK medical staff is comprised of more than 400 of the areas most respected and skilled physicians.

For more than three decades, JFK Medical Center has been a healthcare leader, evaluating the community's needs and expanding services to meet those needs. Services offered include 24-hour emergency care, including a chest pain emergency department and ExpressCare; open-heart surgery; interventional cardiology; electrophysiology arrhythmia disorders; cardiac rehabilitation; bladder control; oncology; inpatient and outpatient surgery; minimally invasive surgery; transitional care; sleep disorders; wound care; pain management; diabetes treatment and education; and comprehensive women's health,

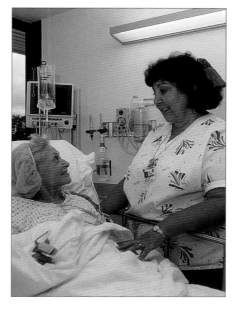

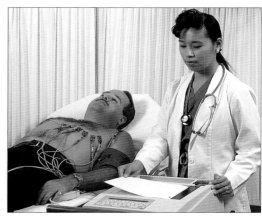

including state-of-the-art advanced breast biopsy imaging (ABBI) services.

The medical center is one of Palm Beach County's primary employers, with a staff of more than 2300. A dedicated Volunteer Auxiliary, with over 500 members, provides support services in a variety of patient care areas.

JFK Medical Center is a proud partner in the Palm Beach County community, offering a wide range of outreach programs, lectures, and health screenings. The facility has forged partnerships with numerous nonprofit organizations such as the American Heart Association, American Cancer Society, American Diabetes Association, Komen Foundation, United Way, The Literacy Coalition and Big Brothers/Big Sisters in an effort to improve the health and quality of life for area residents, employees and the community as a whole.

An affiliate of Columbia/ HCA Healthcare Corporation, JFK Medical Center is fully accredited by the joint Commission on the Accreditation of Healthcare Organizations. In 1995, the facility was named to the prestigious HCIA/Mercer list of the *Top 100 Hospitals in the USA.*

Pictured: (L-R clockwise) Cardiac Rehabilitation, Rothman Center Ambulatory Surgery, Open Heart Surgery Team, Chest Pain Emergency Department.

Bethesda Memorial Hospital was the first hospital built in Southern Palm Beach County. Over the years, it has earned a reputation for providing quality services in a caring manner.

Bethesda Healthcare System

Generations of local families have passed through the doors of Bethesda Memorial Hospital since 1959. Many of the babies and children who were assured a healthy start at Bethesda are now parents themselves. Their parents have in turn taken on the role of grandparents. Only Bethesda's role as a private, community owned not-for-profit hospital providing quality medical service hand-in-hand with individual caring has not changed with time.

Bethesda, located in Boynton Beach, has not only kept pace with the area's growing families and expanding neighborhoods, but with the new technology, treatments and partnerships to meet their needs.

The Comprehensive Cancer Care Center at Bethesda Memorial Hospital, in addition to a full range of aggressive yet safe treatments and diagnostic services, offers one of only a few out-patient stem cell transplant facilities in the United States. New medical frontiers are also being charted through Bethesda's Hyperbaric Medicine and Wound Care Program, which utilizes exciting new technology involving the use of 100 percent oxygen under high pressure.

Generous support from friends and local businesses throughout the community has assisted Bethesda in its mission to provide premium health care, from prevention and treatment through rehabilitation and on-going support. At the same time, the area's

renowned quality of life and growing need for a complete spectrum of medical services, as well as Bethesda's reputation for quality and commitment, has attracted a distinguished medical staff of more than 400 physicians and surgeons, practicing in more than 30 specialty areas.

Bethesda's complete continuum of care includes a: state-of-the-art Emergency Department, Ambulatory Care Unit, (same day surgery) Cardiac Care Services, Center for Advanced Imaging, Behavioral Medicine Center, Vascular Institute, Fitness Center, Rehabilitation Facility, Transitional Care Unit, Home Care Network, Women's Health Services, Maternity

---

Bethesda's Comprehensive Cancer Care Center was the first in the area to offer 3-D Treatment Planning.

Center, FirstBorn Program, Pediatric Unit, Neonatal Intensive Care Unit and Genetic Counseling Services.

Reflecting both a commitment to the community and a new concept in health care, Bethesda Health City was opened. This new "medical mall" offers Palm Beach County one-stop convenience for most out-patient health care services, including family health and walk-in services, same-day surgery and complete eye care, oral surgery, pediatrics, hearing and speech, comprehensive rehabilitation and medical and surgical specialists.

Today, Bethesda Memorial Hospital together with Bethesda Health City and other Bethesda affiliates form the Bethesda Healthcare System. This system was created to meet the growing medical needs of South Palm Beach County with the same quality and care which has been associated with Bethesda Memorial Hospital for decades.

Free education programs, support groups, speakers bureau, year-round community events, a physician referral service and seniors programs have also contributed to Bethesda's national reputation for quality health care as well as its local reputation as a caring neighbor.

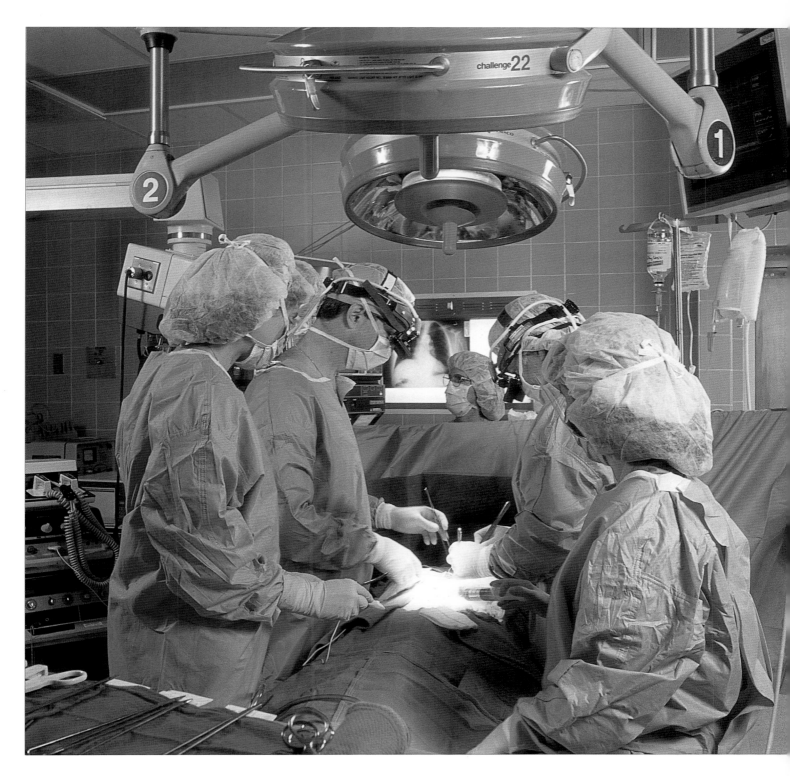

An operating team performs a procedure in one of Palm Beach County's modern surgical suites. Photo Kinsella.

Palm Beach County's Enterprise

Bethesda Memorial Hospital, 202

Boca Raton Community Hospital, 194

Brown Distributing Co., 188-189

Chesterfield Hotel, The, 190

Fairbanks Communications, 193

Florida Atlantic University, 178-179

Florida Crystals, 200

Fran Murphy Interiors, Inc., 180-181

Gulden Real Estate, 192

Hardrives, Inc., 199

Jesse Newman & Associates, 174-175

JFK Medical Center, 201

Judge Knott Center for Historic
    Preservation, 176-177

Lynn University, 184-185

Palm Beach Motor Cars Ltd., 170-173

Palm Beach Post, The, 196

PGA National, 197

Port of Palm Beach, 198

Royal Palm Travel, 195

Ta-Boo, 191

Town Center at Boca Raton, 186-187

Weitz Company, Inc. The, 182-183

General

A

ABC, 104

"Agony in the Garden", 115

Aluminum Corporation of America, 40, 159

Aman Folk Ensemble, 119

American College of Surgeons, 73

Amici, 138

Arden, Elizabeth, 34

Armani, 129

Armory Art Center, 108, 115

Armour, James A. Captain, 14

Army Air Corps, 38

Art in Public Places, 108

ArtiGras, 101

Arvida, 40, 159

Astor, 26, 62

"Au Cafe", 115

B

Backus, A.E. "Beanie", 93

Baker, Robert C. Sheriff, 73, 98

Ballet Florida, 108, 110

Ballet Nacional De Carcas, 119

Barton, Vanderbilt C., 20

Baxter Hall, 95

Beinecke, Walter, 55

Benjamin School, 95

Berlin, Irving, 34

Bethesda Memorial Hospital, 79

Bethesda-by-the-Sea Church, 131

Biddle, Anthony J. Drexel, 31

Blood's Hammock Groves, 58

Board of Control, 91, 92

Boca Raton Community Hospital, 79

Boca Raton Mall, 120

Boca Raton Museum of Art, 103, 120

Boca Raton News, 101, 103

Boca Raton Pops, 120

Boca Raton Resort and Club, 34, 38, 40, 134, 159

Bon Festival, 119

Bonsai, 119

Bookfest, 101

Boynton Beach News, 103

Bradley, E.R. Colonel, 26, 73, 98, 117, 150

Breakers Hotel, The, 26, 38, 75, 136, 150, 151

Breuer, Marcel, 41

Brooks, William "Bill", 105

Brown v Board of Education, 87

Brzoni String Quartet, 117

Buchwald, Art, 117

Buffett, Jimmy, 110

Burt, Ruby, 45

Business Committee for Culture, 108

Butts, Myrtle, 91

C

Cafe Protégé, 136

Caldwell Theatre, 120

Caldwell, Zoe, 120

Callery-Judge Groves, 58, 160

Carrol, Coleman F., Bishop, 94

Catanese, Anthony J., 93

CBS, 104

Center for Creative Education, 108

Central Equities Corporation, 103

Children's Science Explorium, 139

Chiles, Lawton, 134

Christian Science Monitor, 152

CityPlace, 134

Civil Aeronautics Administration, 92

Clematis By Night, 134

Cleveland Symphony Orchestra, 117

Clinton, Bill, 101

Cloister Inn, 34

Cluett Family, 20

CNN, 104

Cocoanut Grove, 26, 150

College of Boca Raton, 95

Colonades Hotel, 159

Colony Hotel, 134

Columbia JFK Medical Center, 79

Columbia/HCA Healthcare Corporation, 79

Community Redevelopment Agency, 120

Conkling, D.H. 98

Connor's Toll Highway, 46, 64

Conway, Joseph, 119

Corts, Paul, 95

Cox Enterprises, 101

Cox, James M. 101

Cragin, Charles I., 20

Creech, Glenwood, 93

Croix, de la, Mother, 94

Cronkite, Walter, 97

Cronyn, Hume, 120

Cultural Executives Committee, 108

D

Davies, Oscar G. 98

Davies, Richard Overrand, 98

Davis, Arthur Vining, 40, 159

Davis, Leonard D. 108

Dawes, Charles, 103

De Leon, Ponce, 20

Delray Community Hospital, 80

Delray Medical Center, 79

Dillman, Hugh, 117

Dimick Family, 14

Dimick, Elisha, "Cap", 14

Dimitri Klien Dance Company, 110

Divoll, Leslie, 118

Dolly Hand Cultural Arts Center, 90, 119

Dreher Park Zoo, 120, 139

Dreyfoos, Alex W. Jr., 105, 108, 110

Du Pont, T. Coleman, 34

DuBois, 53

Duda A. and Sons, 48

Duke, Angier B., 31

Duncan Theatre, 110, 119

E

Eissey, Edward M., 90

El Mirasol, 31

Elliott, Maud Howe, 117

Embassy Club, 117

Estridge, Philip "Don", 40, 64

Everglades Club, 31, 75

Everglades Regional Center, 80

Everglades Research Center, 160

Everglades, The, 45

Evert, Chris, 136

F

Fairbanks, Richard, 104

Fatio, Maurice, 117, 126

Fildes, Frank P., 98

First Bank and Trust Company, 91, 101

"Flagler Divorce Law" 22

Flagler, Alice, 22

Flagler, Henry Morrison Museum, 120, 125

Flagler, Henry Morrison, 20, 22, 31, 40, 62, 98, 99,
    125, 149, 150, 151, 152, 160

Fleming, Thomas F. Jr., 91, 92, 93, 101

Flo-Sun Corporation, 48, 50, 51

Florida Atlantic University, 38, 40, 90, 92, 95, 102

Florida Crystals, 51

Florida Culinary Institute, 136

Florida East Coast Railroad, 150

Florida in the Making, 98

Florida National Guard, 115

Florida Philharmonic Orchestra, 110, 120

Florida State College for Women, 89

Florida State University, 89

Floyd, Chad, 114

Founders Hall, 94

Four Seasons, The, 136

Fyfe, Clyde, 108

G

Gale, Hattie, 84

Garden Club of Palm Beach, 117

"Gardens at Bordighera",

Gauguin, Paul, 115
Geist, Clarence, 34
Glades Auction Market, 55
Glades General Hospital, 80
Good Samaritan Hospital, 73, 75, 80
Gossett, Vivian Rouson, 87
Grace. W.R., 67
Graham, Nancy, 134
Gucci, 129
Gulfstream Polo Club, 136
H
Hale, Marie, 110
Hamilton, James Edward, 16
Hamlisch, Marvin, 110
Hatsume Fair, 119
Heifitz, Jascha, 108
Hendrix, Daniel, 90
Hermes, 129
Hibel Museum of Art, 120
Himmel, Ken, 134
Hispanic Cultural Arts, 108
Howard, E.W. 103
"Huck and Jim on the Mississippi", 119
I
IBM, 40, 41, 64, 67, 102
Indian River Citrus Marketing District, 58
Indian River News, 98
International Museum of Cartoon Art, 120
J
Jacksonville Times Union, 152
Jazz Dance, 119
Joe's Alligator Farm, 28
Johnson, Lyndon B. President, 93
Johnson, Vivian, Residence Hall, 95
Johnson, William, 114
Johnston, Harry, 108
Joques, M. Mother, 94
Jupiter Courier, 103
Jupiter Medical Center, 80
K
Kaiser Color Laboratories, 105
Kelsey, Harry Seymour, 31, 62
Kenan, Mary Lily, 22
King Ranch of Florida, 48, 55
King, William Manley, 115
Kinsey, U.B., 87
Knight Newspapers, 102
Knight Ridder, 102, 103
Kravis, Raymond J. Center, 105, 107, 108, 110,
    114, 129, 134
L
La Vielle Maison, 136
Lake Okeechobee, 42, 44, 45
Lake Worth Herald, 103
Lake Worth News, 98
Lang, August O., 14
Lannan Foundation, 118
Lannan, Patrick J., 118
Lardner, Ring, 150
Lassiter Student Center, 95

"Last Letters from Stalingrad", 119
Leonard, John I., 89
Lighthouse Gallery and School of Arts, 120
Lion Country Safari, 139
"Lonely Planet", 119
Lynn University, 95
Lynn, Christine, 95
Lynn, Eugene, 95
M
Maale, Aileen D., 120
MacArthur, John D. and Katherine T.
    Foundation, 40
MacArthur, John D. State Park, 40, 132
MacArthur, John D., 40, 64, 159
Manor, Harold C., 89
Mar-a-Lago, 126
Marshall, Arthur R. Loxahatchee National Wildlife
    Refuge, 130, 160
Marshall, Thurgood, 87
Marymount College, 94, 95, 119,
McArt, Jan, 120
McCormick, Robert R., 16, 20
McGann, Michelle, 136
Mecca, 53
"Meet Me Downtown" 139
Metcalf, Guy I., 98
Meyer Amphitheater, 134
Miami Ballet Company, 110
Miami Herald, 101, 102, 105
Miami News, 101
Miller, Roger H., 93
Mingei, 117
Mizner Industries, 29, 62
Mizner Park, 120, 134
Mizner, Addison, 28, 29, 31, 34, 38, 62, 64, 75,
    103, 126, 134, 154, 159
Montreal Expos, 136
Montreal Symphony, 117
Moody Bible Institute, 104
Moody, Jess, Reverend, 95
Moore, Charles, 14
Morgan, J.P., 31
Morikami Museum and Japanese Gardens, 119,
    139
Morikami, George Sukeji, 119
Morin, Jim, 120
Morrison Field, 89
Motorola, 64
Mounts Botanical Garden, 118
Munn, 31
Music at Eight, 108
Music at Two, 108
N
National Association for the Advancement
of Colored People, 87
National Endowment for the Arts, 114
National Enquirer, 103
National Museum of Polo and Hall of Fame, 136
NBC, 104
New York Times, 34, 101, 103, 105

New York Tribune, 152
Newsweek, 40
Nicklaus, Jack, 136
"Night Mist", 115
Norman, Greg, 136
Norton Gallery and School of Art, 114
Norton Museum of Art, 95, 107, 114, 115
Norton, Ann, 117
Norton, Ralph Hubbard, 114
O
Office Depot, 67
Old School Square, 120
Orange Grove House of Refuge, 16
Orr-Cahall, Christina, 114
Oshogatsu, 119
P
Palm Beach Atlantic College, 95
Palm Beach Chamber of Commerce, 104
Palm Beach Community College Museum
of Art, 118
Palm Beach Community College, 90, 91
Palm Beach County Convention and
    Visitors Bureau, 159
Palm Beach County Cultural Council, 108
Palm Beach County General Hospital
    Association, 75
Palm Beach County Healthcare District, 80
Palm Beach County School of the Arts, 110
Palm Beach County Workforce   Development
    Board, 68
Palm Beach Daily News, 98, 99, 101, 117
Palm Beach Gardens Artigras, 139
Palm Beach Gardens Medical Center, 79
Palm Beach High School, 87, 110
Palm Beach Inn, 22, 150
Palm Beach International Airport, 38, 68, 108
Palm Beach International Film Festival, 108
Palm Beach Junior College, 87, 89, 90
Palm Beach Life, 98, 99
Palm Beach Opera, 110
Palm Beach Post, 84, 97, 98, 101, 103
Palm Beach Post-Times, 101
Palm Beach Times, 98
Palms West Hospital, 79
Palm View Elementary School, 87
Pan's Garden, 118
Pan of Rohallion, 118
Paramount Theatre, 117
Pathfinder Scholarship Program, 101
Paxson Communications, 105
Paxson, Lowell, "Bud", 105
Pero, 53
Perry, John Holliday, Sr., 98
Philip, Prince, 117
Phipps, Henry C., 31
Phipps Ocean Park, 84
Photo Electronics Corporation, 105, 108, 110
Pierce, Charles, 14
Pierce, Hannibal D., 14
Pierce, Ruby Edna,

Pierce-Moore, Margeretta, 14

Pine Ridge Hospital, 73

Pioneer Life in Southeast Florida, 14

Polk, Willis, 29

Pompey, C. Spencer, 87

Pope, Generoso, 103

Pope, Lois Foundation, 119

Pope, Lois Theatre, 119

Popovich, Helen, 93

Port of Palm Beach, 64, 67

Post, Marjorie Merryweather, 126

Potter, Ellen, 84

Potter, Richard P. Dr., 73

Pratt & Whitney, 64, 67

Pratt, Theodore, 16

Preservation Foundation Ball, 129

Preservation Foundation of Palm Beach, 84

Professional Golfers Association, 40, 136, 159

R

Rapids Water Park, 139

Raspberry, William, 97

Ray, William, 105, 108

RCA, 40

Ream Army Hospital, 38, 75

Red Cross Ball, 128

Red Reef Park, 132

Regional Arts Foundation, 108

Reichenbach, Harry, 154

Religious of the Sacred Heart of Mary, 94

Rinker Hall, 95

Riter, Joseph, 117

Ritter, Rolland, 93

Rockefeller, John D., 20

Rogers, Billy, 53

Rogers, Paul, 92

Roosevelt High School, 89

Roosevelt Junior College for African
   Americans, 87, 89

Roosevelt, Eleanor, 75

Rose, Pete, 136

Rose, Pete, Ballpark Cafe, 136

Royal Palm Dinner Theatre, 120

Royal Palm Sports Club, 136

Royal Palm Yacht and Country   Club, 40

Royal Poinciana Hotel, 22, 26, 149, 150, 151

Royal Poinciana Playhouse, 110, 115

S

Sachs Hall, 95

Safire, William, 97

Sagamore, 14

Saint Andrews School, 95

Sakai, Jo., 119

Schine, Myer J., 40

Schmidt, Charles, 93

Schmidt, Dorothy E. Center for the Arts, 94

Schmidt, Dorothy, 93, 94, 119

Scripps Howard Broadcasting, 103, 105

Second Seminole Indian War, 13

Segel, Floyd A., 114

Sem-Chi, 58

Shannon, Barry C., 98

Shearson, Edward, 31

Shields, Mark, 117

Shiny Sheet, The, 99

Siemans, 64

Singer, Isaac M., 28

Singer, Paris, 28, 29, 31, 73

Smathers, George, 92

Smith, Hedrick, 117

Snyder, Jamie, 120

Society of Arts, 117

Society of the Four Arts, 117

South Bay Growers, 53

South Florida Science Museum, 120, 139

Southern Association of Colleges and
   Schools, 139

Spelling Bee, 101

St. Louis Cardinals, 136

St. Mary's Medical Center, 80

Standard Oil Company, 20, 62

Stockbridge, Frank Parker, 98

Stotesbury, Edward, 31, 62

Stotesbury, Eva, 31

Stronge, William B., 120

Stuttgart Chamber Orchestra, 119

Sugar Cane Growers Cooperative
   of Florida, 48, 50

Sun-Sentinel, 101

Sunfest, 101, 139

Swaidon, Lynda, 110

Swift, George B., 20

T

Ta-boo, 138

Talisman Sugar Corporation, 48

Tenet Healthcare Corp., 79

Testa's, 138

Thatcher, Margaret, Lady, 117

"The Killing of Michael Malloy",119

Thomas, C.A. "Mutt", 53

Tiffany, 129

Tourist Development Council, 159

Trump, Donald, 126

Tucker, Dot, 45, 46

Tucker, Duke, 45

Tucker, Morgan, 45

U

United States Croquet Association, 136

United States Department of Agriculture, 48

United States Life Savings Service, 16

United States Post Office, 41

United States Sugar Corporation, 48, 53

University of Florida College of Architecture, 93

University of Florida Research Station, 52

University of Florida, 92

University of Kentucky, 93

University of South Florida, 92

USA Today, 102

V

Valentines' Day Heart Ball, 128

Valentino, 129

Van Cleef & Arpels, 129

Vanderbilt, 26, 62

Vanderbilt, Harold, 31, 34

Vanderbilt, William K., 34

Veterans Affairs Medical Center, 80

Volk, John L., 117

W

Wackenhut, 67

Walker, Mort, 120

Wall Street Journal, 101, 105

Wanamaker, Rodman, 31, 34

Watkins, Howell Lee, 87, 89

WBZT, 104

WCLB, 104

WEAT-AM, 104

WEAT-FM, 104

Weaver, Ann, Norton Sculpture Gardens, 117

Wedgeworth, George, 50

Wellington News, 103

Wellington Regional Medical Center, 79

West Boca Medical Center, 79

West Palm Beach Auditorium, 108

West Palm Beach Board of Trade, 152

West Palm Beach Boat Show, 139

West Palm Beach Chamber of Commerce, 152

West Palm Beach Fishing Club, 159

WFLA, 103

WFLX, 104

WFOR, 104

"Where Tomorrow Begins", 93

Whitehall, 22, 31, 117

Whitworth, 53

Will, George, 97

Will, Thomas E., 53

Williams, Kenneth Rash, 92, 93

Wilmington College, 94

Wing Chong, 53

"Winter Afternoon", 115

WIRK, 104

WJNA, 104

WJNO, 104

WKGR-FM, 104

WOLL-FM, 104

Worth Avenue, 129

Worth, William Jenkins, Colonel, 13

WPBF, 104

WPBR, 104

WPEC, 104, 105

WPTV, 104, 105

WRLX, 104

WRMB, 104

WRMS, 104

WSVN, 104

WTMI, 105

WTVJ, 104

WXEL, 104

Wyeth, Marion Sims, 114

Y

Yee, 53

Youngblood, Joseph, 87, 89

Photo Dave Sherman.

M.M. Cloutier is an award-winning writer and journalist who has covered virtually all social and economic aspects of South Florida during her career. Her work has been published in magazines, newspapers and journals throughout the country, and she has contributed to the production of three books. She holds a bachelor of arts degree in History and English from the University of North Carolina at Chapel Hill, where she graduated with high honors, and completed advance studies in Spain. For more than a decade she has lived and worked in Palm Beach County.

Barbara Marshall is a West palm Beach freelance writer and video producer. She is the Style editor of the *Palm Beach Daily News*, and writes frequently on lifestyle issues for a variety of regional and national magazines. In addition, she writes and produces videos for a number of corporate clients and government agencies. She was a reporter and anchor for WPBT-TV and WTVJ-TV in Miami, WCPO-TV in Cincinnati and WTVX-TV in Ft. Pierce. She was born in Michigan, grew up in Tampa and has lived in Palm Beach County since 1983.

Stuart B. McIver is the author of ten books on Florida, among them *Yesterday's Palm Beach* and *Hemingway's Key West*, as well as co-author of the 1997 book, *Rating the Presidents*. His other works include the Florida Chronicles — Volume 1, *Dreamers, Schemers and Scalawags*, and Volume 2, *Murder in The Tropics*. In addition he is editor of *South Florida Historical Magazine*, historical writer for the Sun-

Sentinel's Sunshine Magazine and president of the Florida Chapter of Mystery Writers of America. A former resident of Jupiter, he now resides in Lighthouse Point in Broward County.

Thomas J. Schueneman, Ph.D. came to Florida from the staff at Kansas State University where he was in charge of edible crop research at the Wichita Horticultural Research Center. He has been the Cooperative Extension Agent for the Everglades Agricultural Area since 1986. With degrees in fruit and vegetable production, storage and transportation and soil chemistry, he is aptly suited to discuss the agriculture of Palm Beach County. He resides with his wife, Martha, in West Palm Beach.

Millie Wolff attended Journalism School at Ohio State University. Twenty years and three sons later, she graduated from Webster University with a Bachelor of Arts Degree in Mass Communications. Author of many columns in Missouri, Ohio, and Florida newspapers, and books titled *With Love from Grandma* and *Conversations with celebrities*, she is a free lance feature writer in the St. Louis Post Dispatch, Palm Beach Illustrated, Palm Beach Life, Globe Democrat, St. Louis Magazine, and many others. In addition she has been a columnist, feature writer and art editor for the Palm Beach Daily News and a frequent award winner from the Missouri Press Women and Florida Press Women. She is a member of Women in Communications, National Federation of Press Women and the Flagler Rotary.

The appeal of Palm Beach County transcends all ages and time.
Photo Morgan Tyler Photographers.